**build the person**
**you want to be**

Originally a preschool teacher, Simon Rountree has worked across the private, government and not-for-profit sectors in a career that has covered more than 35 years. His work around the mindset required to create stronger mental wellbeing, resilience and meaning within individuals and workforces, and the simple ways of creating this in your life, has been featured in global conferences and publications, as well as the media.

To Jo, Mia, Oliver and a fortunate life.

# build the person you want to be

## the ORANGES toolkit

### simon ROUNTREE

EXISLE
PUBLISHING

'Simon Rountree's *Build the Person You Want to Be* is a welcome addition to the literature on the power of positive psychology and emotional intelligence in transforming individuals to build optimism and resilience whilst generating positive change. Simon outlines a clear and compelling architectural framework for creating the person you want to be, which is refreshingly practical, realistic, flexible and research-based. As someone who has participated in the ORANGES program together with my staff, I can attest to the enormous benefits that utilizing the tools set out in this book will bring in individual and organizational behaviours.'

*John Pender, executive director of the Australian Press Council*

'Inspirational for the aspirational, this book for change provides the tools for those who believe that there is limitless improvement in all of us, based on the premise that positivity can lead to productivity. A must-read for those who wish to lead in all aspects of life.'

*Todd Greenberg, CEO, NRL*

'*Build the Person You Want to Be* represents the opportunity to change the quality of life for an unlimited number of people. There is a large number of tools that are applicable in many different situations and aspects of life, however their power is in their elegant simplicity and practical nature. There are many self-help books and techniques in the world, however the structure and flow of the ORANGES toolkit means it is natural for people to use and adopt, thereby creating lasting positive change in their lives.'

*Paul Findlay, managing director, PD Training*

'Simon's unique and easy to remember ORANGES framework provides a powerful methodology to support leadership development and capability within organizations. Leaders who are passionate about creating sustainable outcomes will discover powerful strategies to get the best out of the most valuable asset an organisation has — its people.'

*Muneesh Wadhwa, founder, Humanity in Business*

First published 2018

Exisle Publishing Pty Ltd
PO Box 864, Chatswood, NSW 2057, Australia
226 High Street, Dunedin, 9016, New Zealand
www.exislepublishing.com

A CiP record for this book is available from the National Library of Australia.

ISBN 978-1-925335-12-5

Designed by Sarah Anderson
Typeset in Adobe Garamond
Printed in China

This book uses paper sourced under ISO 14001 guidelines from well-managed forests
and other controlled sources.

10 9 8 7 6 5 4 3 2 1

The illustration on p. 86 has been adapted from Dwek, C.S. 2007, *Mindset: The new
psychology of success*, Ballantine Books, New York.

**Disclaimer**

# Contents

# Introduction

I'd just been offered a new role as the CEO of a national organization. My negotiations with the board had led me to understand that things weren't great within the organization and that it was facing some major difficulties from a people, financial and business perspective. My brief was clear: for the organization to survive and continue, I'd have to urgently plug the holes to stop the ship from sinking.

With that in mind, the board invited me to attend a special general meeting that had already been called a week prior to my starting date by the organization's stakeholders to address the challenges the organization was facing. The board thought it would be a good opportunity for me to attend, be introduced to people and welcomed to the organization.

After the chairperson had opened the meeting and the formalities were done, the mood within the room quickly turned sour and the agenda went out the window. Of the 200 or so people who were attending, smaller groups formed and started to shout and argue with each other about how to solve the organization's problems and who was to blame. There was an air of anger and frustration within the room, as well as language that was highly negative, suggesting that more bad things were to come. People were being called liars and other names; one of the speakers refused to get up on stage until he received an apology for the name-calling that had been thrown at him, while others who were not down to speak on the agenda were demanding the microphone so they could have a say. At one stage a small group claimed that they weren't been given a chance to be heard and stormed out of the meeting firing abuse at the chairperson and pushing over chairs as they left.

After approximately an hour of listening to people talk over the top of one another, jeer and boo, little seemed to have been achieved. The chairperson, sensing that the meeting needed a new focus, formally introduced me and let everyone know I would be officially starting the following week and that I was looking forward to working with them all.

Now, I'm generally a positive and optimistic person but at this point it's an understatement to say that I was wondering if I'd made the right decision in taking on this role. Everything about the meeting and the way people conducted themselves was disturbing to say the least. The lack of respect, poor attitudes and negative actions simply screamed out to me that maybe I had bitten off more than I could chew. For a moment I thought about running for the hills; however, despite these thoughts I stayed back at the end of the meeting to introduce myself to a number of people who had remained. A few were encouraging, some seemed cautious and others were outright passive aggressive. They either ignored me when I said hello or greeted me with angry comments like:

'If you leave me alone then I'll leave you alone.'

'Don't think you can come in here and tell us what to do.'

'Get out of my face, I have no interest in talking with you.'

My first official day at work was no better — in fact, it was worse. The first few hours were just like anybody's first day: arrive, meet the designated person who shows you around the building, meet the staff and eventually get taken to your office to start the process of getting your head around the job at hand. Several meetings had been organized that day with certain staff and I was in one of these meetings when another colleague interrupted us in a hurried manner, saying that I needed to take a phone call urgently. I left the meeting, picked up the phone and learnt that the person on the other end was from the police department. After introducing himself and providing some background, he informed me that one of the organization's staff had been charged with crimes relating to child safety and welfare.

My stomach dropped. How could this be? This was an organization whose specific purpose was to care for and work with children. How could such an organization not have the right beliefs and attitude to ensure the utmost safety for all? At that moment a clear line was drawn in my mind: for the organization's survival and for the growth of its people there would need to be a complete change in the way our people thought, behaved and acted to ensure the organization never found itself in this situation again.

---

If I fast-forward a number of months, any excitement I felt in taking on a new job had well and truly worn off as I began to unravel the problems and challenges facing the organization. I realized they were far greater than originally explained to me and that the place was even more toxic than what I'd witnessed at that special general meeting. This was a business on the brink of failure.

On the surface the reports, spreadsheets and data (or lack of) showed where the organization was at from a policy and governance perspective. There were lots of quick wins that could be had by putting in place some much-needed business processes and systems. As the months went by, though, I began to understand that the problems we were facing were not actually about our business practices (yes, at the time they were terrible and yes, bringing in new measures would help) but our single biggest challenge was the overall attitude, happiness and wellbeing of our people. The general negativity of our staff was directly undermining or sabotaging the business and this would need to change if the organization was to have any hope of surviving.

Everywhere I looked I saw pessimistic thinking, closed mindsets and a resistance to change and it was clear to me that this had contributed directly to a decline in the operations and values of the business. The culture was toxic, and it showed up in the high staff turnover, poor revenue performance, absenteeism and the fact that almost half of the staff at the time were receiving counselling for stress and anxiety related issues. For many years the staff had done a tremendous job in looking after stakeholders and initially there was never any question as to their commitment and dedication to help the people who used our services. However, even this had declined, as was evident in the recent behaviours and practices that certain people displayed. The organization was in a rut and years of loose leadership and little accountability had allowed people to believe that their destructive behaviours were normal and acceptable. Everywhere I looked I could see the impact of these behaviours and poor thinking habits, which had become ingrained over time. There was an air of low self-esteem within our people and no tools or support to help them shift out of this. The key in turning the situation around would be somehow getting our people to think differently, to see that change was needed and that through a measurable process you could change things for the better. The question was, what would that change look like and how would it happen?

One afternoon after work I was waiting on the side of a football field to pick up my son from training. Another dad was there and we were talking about our day. I was reflecting on how I'd just had one of those days where every staff member seemed to be complaining about something different, there was any number of problems that were brought to me (none with solutions) and they certainly weren't happy and there seemed no one way to fix anything. I asked him how his day had been and he told me that it was similar to mine. Being a builder I thought he was talking about his tradespeople; however, when he said that his complaints didn't talk to him and often he would stumble across them I had to ask what he meant. He went on to explain that he is constantly challenged with problems and that each one had their own complaint and each one was different, so they needed a different tool to fix them — a hammer for this, a saw for that and a screwdriver for something else. He said that there were some tools that could do multiple things but there was never one tool that could do everything. Given that in his line of work he never knows about a problem until he comes across it, he therefore has to carry his tools with him as he never knows what he will need when.

That conversation got me thinking. How had we got into the situation at work where everywhere we turned we seemed to have problems but no solutions, people were constantly complaining, they struggled to deal with everyday challenges and adversities, they kept to themselves and didn't share information and if something good happened, they'd find a way to turn it into a negative?

Each morning when I greeted people and asked how they were, most replied with something along the lines of:

'I could be better.'

'What do you think?'

'Don't ask, I'm flat out.'

Or my favourite: 'Not bad.'

Well if they weren't bad then why didn't they say they were good?

These responses, and the negative thinking behind them, had become a habit and I was sure they weren't even conscious of how they were saying things and the negative language they were using. One thing I did know was that these responses created a negative mood that commenced at the start of the day and carried through to the end. It was no wonder that people and the organization as a whole felt flat.

I was trying to understand why our people were like this when I came across this poem, which to me perfectly summed up our situation:

> You may know me. I am your constant companion.
>
> I am your greatest helper; I'm your heaviest burden.
>
> I will push you onward or drag you down to failure.
>
> I am at your command.
>
> Half the tasks you might do might as well be turned over to me. I am able to do them quickly and I am able to do them the same every time if that's what you want.
>
> I am easily managed — all you have to do is be firm with me.
>
> Show me exactly how you want it done, and after a few lessons I'll do it automatically.
>
> I am the servant of all men and women; of course, I am the servant of the failures as well.
>
> I've made all the great people who have ever been great. And I've made all the failures, too.
>
> I work with the precision of a marvellous computer, with the intelligence of a human being.

You may run me for profit or you may run me to ruin, it makes no difference to me. Take me, be firm with me and I'll put the world at your feet. Be easy with me and I will destroy you.

Who am I?

And there it was — habit. With the answer staring me in the face I knew we had to look at and start creating better, more positive habits that would support our people's thinking and help us create the culture we needed to turn around the business. Habits that would support personal growth and allow people to show more positive behaviour than negative.

So something had to change in the thinking habits of our people but I didn't know how this could be done. I honestly believe that people generally want to look at what is right with life rather than what is wrong. Surely people prefer their life to have more joy than sorrow, more hope than despair?

However, if it was that easy to do then why weren't they doing it? I figured the reason must have been that without the knowledge to understand and change a habit it's easier to ignore it. I decided that we needed to work on creating tools that would give people the ability to create good new thinking habits, but at that stage I didn't have the science or knowledge to show people how.

## Habits and the brain

There's a lot of scientific research around habits — what are they, how they're formed and how to break them. In simple terms, there are four parts to the brain. The brain stem at the back of our skull controls functions such as breathing, heart rate and blood pressure. The amydgala is shaped like an almond and lies deep within our brain, responding to our basic survival needs such as the fight or flight response. The cerebellum, in the middle of our skull, looks after things such as our balance, coordination and movement, to name a few. The cerebrum, at the front of our skull, is important as it's made up of lots of lobes that look after things such as our thinking, our problem-solving and our habits.

One major benefit of having a habit is that it allows the conscious part of our brain to go exploring while the unconscious part of the brain gets on with doing the boring, repetitious things in life. For example, how often do you actually think about the physical movements required to tie up your laces when you put on a pair of shoes? Most of us just do this automatically, as we have trained our brain over a period of time to create a lifelong habit. The other benefit of habits is that they protect us from 'decision fatigue' so that our brain doesn't get overloaded, lose energy and suffer mental fatigue from simply having to make too many decisions. The brain likes us to have habits. Whatever we can train ourselves to do automatically, the brain will accept so it can be freed up to focus on other things. The brain makes no distinction between good or bad habits — that part is up to us.

Habits generally operate in a cycle known as the Habit Cycle or Habit Loop. The cycle can be easily described as follows:

+ **Trigger.** A sign that tells your brain which habit to use.
+ **Routine.** The mental, physical or emotional habit you use without even thinking about it. These can be either good or bad.
+ **Reward.** Helps your brain figure out if the habit is worth remembering for the future.

Through repetition we strengthen the neural pathways in our brain. The repetition involved in doing something over and over again forms a cycle that simply becomes a habit. The association of the trigger and behaviour become so connected to the reward that it creates a commanding habit that won't be broken unless you retrain your brain to do so.

Generally, if you want to shift a habit the trigger and reward stay the same but it is the routine that needs to change for you to have any chance of changing.

It's important to stress that changing habits is easily described but not necessarily easy to do. Some habits are harder to change than others and there is no universal approach or magical set number of days required to form a new habit. A general rule of thumb is that establishing or breaking a habit and therefore creating a new routine can take anywhere from twenty to 200 days, sometimes more, sometimes less, depending on what it is that you're trying to do. For example, training yourself to eat a piece of fruit with lunch each day may be an easier habit for you to form than starting an exercise program by going for a jog each morning before breakfast. In his book *Making Habits, Breaking Habits*, psychologist Jeremy Dean states that it can take, on average, 66 days to form a new habit, with easier habits taking 21 days and much harder ones taking hundreds of days.[1] No matter what the number of days, the fact remains that it takes a lot of practice to implement and accomplish a new routine.

## The Habit Cycle in practice

With this in mind, I looked at the habits and behaviours of our people and the organization and sought advice from experts in the field of psychology, in particular positive psychology. From the evidence-based research that was available and as a first step, a conscious effort was made to look at and change the environments we were working in to improve the behaviours of our people and to allow for greater communication and engagement. We wanted to make real change and were looking for some quick wins to create a happier, more positive atmosphere and improve the ambience of our workplace. So we painted the walls in vibrant colours, decluttered and removed partitions to allow more natural light to filter through. After some initial push-back from staff it very quickly became apparent that their working environment could be made more pleasurable and workable for them, their teams and the whole organization. In the greater scheme of things it might seem like a small win, but from a psychological perspective it was a huge signal that change was possible, that change could be a good thing and that habits could be shifted.

I also wanted to look at certain habits that some people had, that were really not benefiting the organization. I worked with them to understand, challenge and change their own behaviours. For example, one particular senior staff member disliked attending managers' meetings and would spend most of her time acting bored while looking at her mobile phone or laptop, rarely contributing anything of significance. It helped me to understand her behaviour if I looked at it through the lens of the Habit Cycle.

The trigger for her habit was having to attend a managers' meeting. The routine was that she would distract herself from having to be mentally part of the meeting (although she could say that she always attended as she was physically present) by spending time checking her emails or looking at the internet on her phone or laptop. The reward for her was that she believed this allowed her to be seen as a team player by physically being present, but by not engaging in the meetings or committing she couldn't be held responsible for anything.

The impact of this was that all the other managers in the meeting would get frustrated at this person's behaviour and lack of engagement and wonder why she even bothered to turn up at all. Something had to change as the meetings were unproductive and the resulting tension meant it was getting to the point where no one wanted to attend!

With my direct leadership team on board, we decided to make a few changes to the managers' meetings to see if we could shift the routine of this person and others. We hoped in time to move her from a habit that was being unhelpful and disruptive to one that would be engaged and productive. First, a rule was made that no one was allowed to bring a laptop or mobile phone into the meeting unless it had some direct relevance to that meeting's agenda, e.g. they had a Power Point presentation or spreadsheet to display. Second, the role of the chairperson for the meeting was rotated among all the managers to ensure that everyone had to contribute and take responsibility for being part of a team. A checklist guide was created for the chairperson to follow so they would have the authority to make decisions that would work best for the team and have the responsibility of driving that meeting's agenda, as well as seeking input from all participants and ensuring the meeting achieved actions and outcomes that would support the organization.

Initially the responses from the manager in question were fairly typical for someone reluctant to change, with comments such as not being able to take your mobile phone into a meeting was stupid, but she quickly realized we were serious when we elected her to chair the first meeting. For her the trigger was the same each time — attending a managers' meeting — and the reward was fairly similar, in that she would still be seen as a team player (in fact more so, as she was actually contributing rather than just turning up) and the meetings now allowed her to get on with 'actual' work.

It's fair to say that the changes in this manager's habit didn't happen overnight but they did happen over a couple of months, to the point where she became a very strong and integral part of the team. She would turn up to meetings on time, put up her hand to take on certain actions arising from the meeting and also support others with their actions. She grew into and enjoyed the added responsibility of chairing meetings and learning about other parts of the business while collectively working for the same outcomes.

Over time, by simply changing the routine this person was taken from being unproductive and unsupportive of team meetings to becoming fully engaged and connected.

Other things we implemented included starting every meeting with a joke, a fun activity or a positive message. An activity called 'fun therapy' was created that allowed people to stop work to play a game such as who could fly a paper aeroplane the furthest or a trivia competition, and successes were celebrated by ringing a cymbal that hung from the ceiling every time something good happened. All of these were designed to create strong and tangible symbols to fundamentally change the routine of how the organization operated and they required lots of practice and repetition. They were good from a collective and team perspective, but we were still missing a key ingredient which focused on the individual and gave them the tools that, through practice, would change their routine and in turn support a good habit to enhance their overall wellbeing. We'd made a start, but changing people's thinking and attitudes was going to take time and require some more robust evidence-based tools.

## Building a toolkit for positive change

I started to read every management, research and business book I could get my hands on. They all had pearls of wisdom but mostly focused on process, procedures and profits, and very little on people and the tools necessary to enhance their wellbeing, or how as a leader I could drive the link between wellbeing and performance.

I then came across some research by Barsdale and Gibson that stated, 'The evidence is overwhelming that experiencing and expressing positive emotions and moods enhances performance at individual, group and organizational levels'.[2]

I had a 'lightbulb moment'. In order to enhance the wellbeing of our people we had to look at how we could improve and enhance positive emotions and moods on a daily basis and give people the tools to create these good habits. Because we were serious about improving performance and our business outcomes, we also had to be able to measure these so that people could not only feel the difference but see it as well, through a diagnostic tool. And that also meant we could track if what we were doing was actually making a difference.

This was the key I was looking for and I started exploring positive psychology research undertaken by people such as Martin Seligman, Deborah Danner, Michael Lemonick and others. From this I quickly learnt that people with higher levels of wellbeing are:

+ healthier
+ have stronger immune systems
+ live longer
+ are more tolerant of pain
+ are more resilient
+ recover quicker from illness
+ are socially more engaged.

All of these outcomes are supported by a fundamental theory by Barbara Fredrickson, a leading Professor of Psychology at the University of North Carolina, whose main work relates to the Broaden and Build theory of positive emotions. This theory indicates that positive emotions expand cognition and behavioural tendencies and have the capacity to expand or broaden our thinking (they literally grow our thinking) while they build our personal resources.

Fredrickson stated that, 'Positive emotions do more than make us feel good, they also expand our thinking, help us generate new ideas and encourage us to consider other possibilities'.[3]

The research shows that expanding positive emotions allows us to build our own:

+ intellectual resources (our cognitive capacity)
+ physical resources (our immune system)
+ social resources (being with people)
+ psychological resources (resilience and emotional management).

So positive emotions have a strengthening and enhancing impact on our brain and bodies on multiple levels. Fedrickson's research shows that positive emotions allow our brain to remain calm, think more clearly and function better. They allow our bodies to recover quicker from illness and heal faster from injury, as well as better handle the stress and adversity in our lives. And they support us in strengthening our relationships and communications with others and within communities. Fredrickson's Broaden and Build theory has been supported by multiple studies and research into health, wealth, pain management, business and many other areas.[4–7]

Once I read this my mind went back to the conversation I'd had that evening with my builder friend on the side of the football field, and I reflected on how he carried around his tools and had different tools for different challenges. It was at this moment that I realized in order for our people to significantly change their mindsets, behaviours, habits and overall wellbeing, we had to give them the necessary tools to carry around with them on a daily basis to broaden their thinking and build their resources. These tools needed to be research-based, practical in application, sustainable, measurable and clearly support them in building a happier and healthier life.

It was at this point that I started to imagine a toolkit for positive change and to think about what essential tools would be required in the kit. The tools could have a specific purpose or be multipurpose, but I knew even then that there certainly wouldn't be one tool for all occasions.

Given that the general feeling at work was such that bad things were more likely to happen than good, we certainly needed to start by shifting people's general thinking from pessimism to optimism. We needed our people to be able to see the path they were on and have the skills to navigate around any barriers in their way. The research on this clearly showed that you can learn strategies to be more optimistic, so an optimism tool was definitely going to be the first tool in the kit.

The toolkit was in its very early stages but my vision was starting to take shape. I was constantly on the lookout for new practical tools that could be added, and given the amount of challenges our people faced it didn't take long for other scenarios to present themselves and show me what was needed. At a regular staff meeting one day it dawned on me that there was a common thread in these meetings. There was a feeling of hopelessness or defeat in the air that carried forward from one week to the next. It was true the organization had gone through a difficult and traumatic period and our people faced numerous challenges and adversities on a regular basis, but there was a complete lack of resilience.

This was emphasized when one of our managers announced at the meeting that he hadn't prepared a sales report and therefore had missed a deadline for important financial information to be processed. Further to this he would no longer be following up people to purchase tickets in a fundraising activity we were holding, as they would simply say no and he was tired of people saying no to him, even though it was his job to make sales and raise money. His capacity to withstand stress or adapt well to the challenge he faced completely overwhelmed him to the point he simply gave up. It was no wonder the organization was going downhill fast. If people whose role it was to make sales and generate revenue were giving up then what hope did we have of making any money at all? In order to survive we needed to build our resilience and foster the ability to bounce back more effectively from whatever adversity would come our way.

One morning a staff member arrived at the office complaining that the day was going to be nothing but hard work. He had a long list of things to be done and in his mind he was the only one who could do them. His abrasive behaviour and loud language was impacting others, so I took him aside for a quiet word. Initially he couldn't see the wood from the trees — he believed he had a mountain of work that just kept piling up which nobody but him could do and everything was a priority. After some minutes of talking we determined that not all the tasks he deemed a priority needed to be completed that day, and that there were actually other people who could assist him in ensuring that all deadlines could be met without a negative impact on others. In this situation, the staff member's attitude when he arrived at work was that it would be a bad day no matter what, and this influenced his behaviour and communication, and his negativity spread to others around him. If things were going to improve then people need to have the tools to create a much more positive attitude. Therefore, attitude became the next tool required for the toolkit.

As I learned more about the benefits each of these tools offered I started to see how important having a toolkit would be and was excited about the possibilities that learning skills in one area (e.g. optimism) would also broaden the thinking and build skills in another area (e.g. resilience).

Our people always seemed to be complaining about how busy they were but couldn't clearly articulate what they were busy doing. Staff would leave meetings to take what seemed to be an endless procession of 'urgent' phone calls then return huffing and puffing that they had just got more work to do. People would turn up late to a meeting or without the appropriate materials or papers. When people were there you could see that they didn't listen and only contributed when an agenda item had some relevance to them. The organization and its people all worked independently, thinking and complaining about what happened or possibly would happen in the future; no one was actually present in the moment or aware of the impact they were having on each other. It seemed they were simply passing through that moment on the way to something else without even realizing it. The crazy thing was that some people had some really good successes to share or things to contribute to the meeting, but no one really heard or acknowledged them as their minds were anywhere but in that room. There was no chance of us individually or collectively getting traction as everyone's lack of focus was counter to what we were trying to achieve which, ironically, was focus. We needed a tool to help people be in the 'now', be mindful and focused so that they could be aware of conversations, behaviours and surroundings. The tool needed to provide people with the ability to have richer experiences, notice more and have greater emotional control and to focus on enjoying the present moment, rather than being mindless. And so we designed a mindfulness tool we called 'Now'.

The organization had been around for approximately twenty years and in that time it claimed that its people came first and business second. However, it was obvious that recently there was no clarity around who or what came first, and repeated challenges, failures and hardships had put the organization in a perilous state. Along with all the negative talk and actions that had become a normal part of our everyday workplace, people had lost the art of being thankful. Very rarely did people share or celebrate success, either big or small, and rarely did people acknowledge a good deed or offer of support. No one ever acknowledged that gratitude could support them in being able to live a happier life or that although we might not be grateful for hardships, we certainly can find gratitude within them. Our toolkit therefore needed a gratitude tool, one that could support the quality of being thankful and instil a readiness to show appreciation for, and to return, kindness. The importance of this tool was also to give people an understanding that real gratitude is, at times, confronting and painful but by accepting certain realities about a situation you can find an opportunity to be thankful. People within the organization were in this exact situation: they all had challenges and by learning the skill of gratitude we hoped we they would be able to see their challenges from a new perspective and appreciate the opportunity to learn and grow. This tool needed to work alongside our attitude tool and together they could prove to be a powerful combination to broaden our thinking and build our personal resources.

I mentioned earlier how the organization and its people were flat and lethargic. I really started to believe that the energy or enjoyment levels (or should I say lack of excitement) were having a powerfully negative impact. Early one morning I received a call from a new staff member who asked me if I would mind if she worked from home that day as she thought she could be more productive away from the office. She went on to say that she looked forward to coming to work but when she got there she started to lose her zest, feel overwhelmed and felt that she was a sponge for other people's negative energy. This staff member had the empathy for the challenges the organization faced and had come into the role with her eyes wide open; however, what was not taken into consideration was the simple fact that the constant lack of enjoyment and low levels of enthusiasm portrayed by the majority of people was draining. When I got off the phone I went for a walk around the office — the only sound you could hear was the tapping of keyboards as people sat at their computers. There was no talk, certainly no laughter and people's posture demonstrated lethargy. I'm not saying that people weren't working, but the environment they were contributing to was certainly not conducive to engaging and meaningful work.

Generally speaking, work means more to us than just a pay cheque. It gives us a connection to society and reality, and is more important to us than most people give it credit. It helps us make friends, meet different people, learn new skills, be part of a team, earn money, buy things and a host of other benefits. We spend a large part of our week and life working, so surely it would be better to enjoy what you do and aim to contribute to an engaged work environment. If you're not happy in your role and your perception is that work is bad, then more than likely it is bad and more than likely this will have an impact in some way on other parts of your life. I started to wonder how long people had been behaving like this, training their brains to deliver tensions, sadness and low energy to their bodies. The toolkit would need to have an energy tool that could create a tipping point for us and help people feel less stressed and anxious while being more energized and excited about life. I could start to see how this energy tool would complement other tools in our kit to broaden our thinking around Optimism, Attitude, Resilience, Now and Gratitude. The toolkit was almost complete but there was still one more essential tool missing.

The final tool we were looking for needed to be very specific, one that individuals could relate to, was tangible and could be used and practised every day.

The part of people's personalities that displays positive actions and thoughts is known as strengths. Understanding and working with these strengths can create pathways for developing a happier, more engaged and healthier life. Strengths are an established way of behaving, thinking or feeling that is authentic and energizing to the individual. Playing to our strengths also enables us to optimize our performance. In other words, strengths bring out the best in each of us and can be applied across all aspects of our lives. It became clear to me how important this final tool would be, as once an individual had an understanding of their strengths they could utilize them in supporting their optimistic- and resilience-based tools as well. If we could help people identify, understand and maximize their strengths they could potentially become happier and more productive at home, in the community and, of course, at work. In this way we hoped to unlock the potential within our staff, our teams and the organization.

The toolkit was now complete. It contained enough practical tools and proven strategies to help a person flourish by increasing their level of positive emotions, therefore helping them move closer to a more engaged and meaningful life. The toolkit would give people strategies to build a number of psychological and social resources to help them cope with life's challenges, no matter how big or small. It would help them feel good and maintain a more balanced life and put the brakes on the possibility of negativity dragging them down and keeping them there.

With all this in place we simply had to come up with a name for the toolkit. One day when I was training for a major trekking expedition, the name fell into place. Day after day, with my backpack on, I would walk for hours up and down an extremely steep hill near my house to build up my level of fitness. I had been doing it long enough to get to know the neighbours in the houses that I would walk past on the way up and down, and they would often offer me words of encouragement. Even though walking up and down the same hill for hours may have seemed crazy to them, it gave me a great opportunity to practise the tools in the toolkit. I was able to be present in the moment, keep completely focused on the task at hand

and appreciate the things around me. It certainly built up my levels of resilience as I trained in all types of weather and often my tired and aching body would cry out to stop and go home but I had to push through as I knew there would be no stopping or going back once I was in the jungle.

At the time life was very busy with the challenges at work, juggling family commitments and attempting to train for this trek but I decided that I would bring a positive attitude and high energy levels to every situation, as I knew by then that this would influence my behaviour and communication. I wanted to look at all the things I was juggling at work and home, together with this adventure I was training for, with a more solution focused, can-do approach, rather than the can't approach that had been happening at work. That's not to say that everything went well all the time or that I had a Pollyanna view on life but certainly the optimistic thinking resources I used gave me a tendency to believe that a good outcome would be achieved in most situations.

In the final days of my training I went out to do one last big workout. By then I'd built up the stamina to tackle the steep hill in a much more determined manner. A number of people in the street knew my day of departure was soon and at various times during the final workout they came out to wish me well. I must have looked a real sight in my trekking gear with backpack on in the middle of suburbia sweating like I had just taken a shower. One elderly neighbour brought out an ice-cold jug of water for me and some freshly cut up fruit and I stopped for ten minutes to have a drink and a chat. I was extremely grateful for this lady's gesture as her cool water was far more soothing and seemed to quench my thirst far better than the water I was carrying, which had warmed up in the day's heat. When I thanked her, she surprised me by saying that she was the one who should be thanking me as our little talks over the months had made her curious to learn about the place I was heading to and the people who live there, so she had taken the time to find out and learn. She went on to say that if we hadn't met she may never have known what she found out and that her life was a little bit richer for that knowledge. In saying goodbye I grabbed the last bit of fruit and stuck it in my mouth. It was an orange cut in quarters with the skin still on and I put it over my teeth like a mouthguard. It was during this moment that I thought about the names of the tools in the toolkit and imagined the first letter of each. Sure enough, the name ORANGES came out. It was there on the side of this very steep hill in the final days of my training that the ORANGES toolkit got its name.

# What makes ORANGES different?

The world is full of self-help books claiming how to make us better people or how to create more meaning in our lives, and to some people this book may be seen as just another one of those. Thanks to the thousands of options on the internet and social media we are now led to believe that our long-term happiness, health and wellbeing could possibly be only a few clicks away. Many of the self-help programs these days claim to have the solution: some encourage you to search within yourself, while others claim they can magically transform your life and try to either sell you a new elixir, help you create space in an overloaded world of communication and technology, tell you there is a special secret you should know about or focus on fixing your weaknesses to magically transform your life. We also live in a world that seems to promote the idea that wellbeing is to be found through wealth, fame, good looks or talent and that without them you can't find happiness. Sadly, much of this information is generated from 'happiness gurus', life coaches, various media outlets or an individual's personal perspective without much academic substance. With so much choice and with so much conflicting information, how are we able to work out which option will be the one that works?

The best way to make choices is to look for the intellectual and practical data, evidence and research that supports the claim that is being made. In other words, look towards the science and the body of knowledge that it supports on that particular subject.

This is where ORANGES is different. ORANGES is not a magic solution, nor is it something you simply dream about. It's a research-based wellbeing program built on the science and practices of positive psychology. It is founded on the belief that people want to have meaningful lives and nurture what is best within themselves to enhance their experiences of play, love and overall wellbeing whether at home, at work or in the community.

ORANGES is not about identifying a problem, understanding the cause of the problem, then looking for a solution to alleviate its negative impact. It takes a different perspective — it focuses on the scientific study and verifiable observations of what makes humans flourish, and groups together the individual key elements known to enhance our strengths and emotions to enable us to thrive. The point is that ORANGES is not about achieving perfection and being flawless in our lives, nor does it ask you to be happy and optimistic all the time no matter what the circumstances. Life generally places many pressures on us, so to add an expectation that you must be happy all the time is unrealistic and bound to fail. ORANGES is simply about learning the skills and tools to allow you to thrive and flourish, to bounce back from the challenges and adversities that come our way. It supports you to focus on what's working well in your life and helps you determine how you can make it work even better.

ORANGES offers seven key principles, based on research-proven techniques and empirical studies, to improve your overall wellbeing, optimism and performance. It provides practical tools that can be applied to everyday life. It teaches you skills to prevent and reduce stress-related problems such as anxiety, burn-out and attrition, while supporting positive attributes such as performance, broader thinking and gratitude. And the best thing about it is that it's measurable.

I certainly hope that by using the tools provided you will, over time, see the benefits and feel happier for it, but at no stage is it claimed that ORANGES is the sole answer to your or others' problems. It's not a quick-fix solution; improving your overall wellbeing takes time and practice. In fact, if you've been suffering prolonged bouts of sadness, disgust, anger, fear or if you have any mental health concerns you should consult a health professional. Also, I would like to note that there needs to be sufficient individual foundation stones in place, such as food and shelter, for people to be able to thrive. Trying to improve your wellbeing in the absence of these is extremely difficult, as your life is marked by the struggle to simply meet your basic needs.

ORANGES does, however, give you lots of science-based and well-researched tools which, if practised, used and turned into a habit, will improve and add value to your overall wellbeing. It will simply broaden your thinking and build your personal toolkit.

The key differences of ORANGES are:

+ it is research based
+ it will give you useful tools
+ it's measurable
+ it can be done as a whole or in segments.

# It is research based

To date, the research undertaken within the positive psychology field has covered areas including positive health, resilience, learned helplessness, purpose and meaning, gratitude, energy, positive emotions, positive neuroscience and flourishing. Along the way, the scientific research has identified a number of key universal philosophies for human happiness and improved wellbeing, which know no boundaries of age, religion or ethnicity. The ORANGES program takes the foundations of these philosophies and the findings of worldwide research in order to increase our knowledge of positive emotions, engagement and meaning. Whether it is particular research on optimism, resilience, attitude or any of the other letters in ORANGES, these bodies of work provide the evidence and facts to support and build better mindsets and behaviours to improve our overall wellbeing.

# It will give you useful tools

At the completion of ORANGES you will have the knowledge to use and implement individual tools across seven different areas of positive psychology that have been proven to enhance wellbeing. You don't have to use every tool, just pick the ones that work for you. All of the tools have been designed for ease of use and most require nothing more than your memory for them to be implemented. There is no need to purchase any new equipment or acquire anything else beyond what you currently have at your disposal, as part of the key to their success is in their simple application.

As you work through the book, you might discover that you are already using some of these tools and, if so, keep using them. Others might be new to you, and if this is the case then remember to practise, practise and practise so that they become a good habit and so ingrained in your brain that you don't have to think about using them. All the tools in this book take time to master and will work differently for different people. Initially, try choosing the ones that are the easiest for you to implement and then build from there. Life isn't perfect and neither are these tools, so don't worry about making mistakes or losing enthusiasm to practise. Simply start again.

## It's measurable

With ORANGES you can measure your progress across each of the key elements that support your overall wellbeing. By initially undertaking each of the inventories found at the end of each chapter, you can establish a score of where you are currently at across the ORANGES principles. Then by practising and using on a regular basis the tools that are best suited to you, you can remeasure yourself over a period of time (three, six, nine or twelve months later) and see if your score has changed. You might be surprised at what you find.

## It can be done as a whole or in segments

You can choose to do all seven areas of ORANGES or just the ones that interest you. However, the benefit of doing all seven is that they are interlinked and from this you will see how gratitude is linked to optimism and resilience, attitude to energy, etc. The potential to improve your overall wellbeing increases significantly by undertaking the whole program, as not only will you have a greater knowledge and skill set to broaden your thinking but you will have more tools at your disposal. I would therefore encourage you to attempt each letter of ORANGES. However, for those who may want to, for example, just do resilience or strengths then there is nothing stopping you doing so and achieving benefits in that particular area.

This program will give you the science, research and evidence-backed data to broaden your knowledge base and support your overall wellbeing. You will have a large toolkit at your disposal, full of proven, practical tools that, when applied with balance and rigour on a regular basis, will enhance your life. Further to this you can measure your progress and the impact these tools have on you. And you'll be empowered to decide how much or how little you want ORANGES to be part of your life.

# Positive psychology

As Barbara Fredrickson stated, 'Positivity transforms us for the better. By opening our hearts and minds, positive emotions allow us to discover and build new skills, new ties, new knowledge and a new way of being.'[1]

The following outlines just some of the many studies undertaken that support the case of ORANGES.

## Individual wellbeing

Research shows that people with higher levels of wellbeing experience a wealth of positive benefits. An international meta-analysis comprising of more than 200 studies involving 275,000 people discovered that happiness levels steer us to better achievements in almost every life domain such as health, energy, longevity, social connection and learning capacity. And that happiness, positive moods and emotions are an essential part of achieving success, not merely a by-product of it.[2]

## Positive emotions

Positive effect is critical to the growth of individuals and teams within an organization. Research shows that positive emotions have a progressive impact within organizations from a performance, decision making, turnover, prosocial behaviours, negotiation and conflict resolution, group dynamics and leadership perspective.[3]

## Healthier, stronger immune system

Research shows that happiness, optimism and contentment may reduce the risk or limit the severity of issues such as cardiovascular and pulmonary diseases, diabetes, hypertension and colds.[4] Further, it has been found that people who, when tested, rate highly for happiness develop about 50 per cent more antibodies than those who do not rate so well.[5] Also, research showed that cancer survivors with more uplifting experiences have enhanced natural killer (NK) cell activity and greater resistance to infection than those who had more hassles and stress in their lives.[6]

## Increase income and success

Research has found that people who are naturally happier score higher on management effectiveness tasks and have greater success in areas such as leadership and mastery of information.[7] As a result of being more likely to get promoted, these individuals achieve higher salaries, and bigger and more frequent bonuses.[8]

## Cultivate creativity

A study by psychologist Robert Epstein showed that despite a widely held belief that some people just aren't endowed with a creativity gene, there is no real evidence that demonstrates one person is inherently more creative than another, and that the ability to cultivate creativity is something that anyone can achieve and make a habit.[9]

## Increased pain tolerance and resilience

A study was conducted where participants were asked to hold their hands in a bucket of freezing ice for as long as possible. Those who were found, via testing, to have higher levels of happiness and wellbeing were able to hold their hands in the bucket for much longer than those who had scored lower on the same test.[10]

## Living longer

According to a Dutch study of elderly patients, upbeat mental states reduced an individual's risk of death by 50 per cent over the study's nine-year duration.[11] And in a survey of people living in industrial countries, happier people were found to enjoy an increased longevity of between seven-and-a-half and ten years.[12] Happier people are less likely to commit suicide, and they are less often the victim of accidents.[13]

## Care and altruism

Research suggests that altruism may follow from happiness and vice versa. Researchers following a large sample of volunteers found those with high levels of wellbeing and life satisfaction invested more hours in volunteer activities over the course of the study. At the same time, those who volunteered more hours increased their happiness.[14]

## Social engagement

Many studies demonstrate the link between high levels of happiness and the actual number of friends or companions people report, as well as the social support and companionship they experience and perceive. This is not surprising when you consider that relationships are considered by scientists as the most important factor in our survival as a species.[15]

## Happiness and organizational effectiveness

Businesses with high employee wellbeing report greater customer loyalty and satisfaction, higher rates of employee retention and attendance, higher productivity and higher profits.[16,17]

Further studies linking happiness with productivity show that people who are naturally happy score higher on management effectiveness tasks. When people are in a good mood they tend to solve problems faster, more collaboratively and more creatively. Happy leaders receive higher ratings from customers and are more likely to have happier and healthier employees.[18]

# The ORANGES program

# 1

# Optimism

**Optimisim** (*noun*) A tendency to expect the best possible outcomes or dwell on the most hopeful aspect of a situation.

> Our greatest weakness lies in giving up. The most certain
> way to succeed is always to try just one more time.
>
> **Thomas Edison**

Martin Seligman, a leading figure in the field of positive psychology, states that optimistic people believe the adversity, challenges or negative events they face are temporary, that they can be managed and that there are limits as to how much such events will impact their lives. He defines optimism as a skill that provides an individual with a sense of confidence and ability to overcome the problems they face.

If we are optimistic we tend to look at life from a solution-focused perspective. That's not to say optimistic people wear rose-coloured glasses or have a Pollyanna view of the world. Blind optimism is not what is meant by the above definition. It's about being able to see the rocks in the road yet having the belief that you have the skills to navigate a path either around, over, under or through them.

Some people believe you are born either pessimistic or optimistic and often fall in to the trap of labelling people in this manner: 'Trust Mary to say that, she was positive even in the cradle'; 'Just my luck, nothing ever goes right for me'. However, this a myth. Optimism is an explanatory style — that is, the way in which we explain to ourselves events or circumstances. And being an explanatory style, optimism therefore moves and shifts depending on what's happening at the time. Like other thoughts in our brain, it's subject to neuroplasticity, the brain's amazing potential to change and adapt as required. Neurons are nerve cells that process and transmit information and they are an important part of the brain's ability to restructure itself. Think of training your brain to do something new, such as learning a musical instrument or teaching yourself to juggle. When learning a musical instrument at first everything seems awkward and uncomfortable. You often hit the wrong note and your fingers don't seem to be very coordinated with what your brain is telling them to do. Each wrong note may create an opportunity to distract you or create the thought in your mind that it was a bad idea to take up this instrument. However, the more you practise the more comfortable and coordinated you become and the fewer wrong notes you hit. Continued practise forges new connections (known as neural pathways) in your brain that, in this example, are related to playing music. You find that you start to think less and less about the movements you have to do until finally the noise and distortion in your head is gone and you mentally get the right frequency and play a piece of music without fault. You can think of building new neural pathways the same way when learning anything new. The more you focus and practise something, the stronger those neural pathways become and the better you get at the new skill you are learning or the challenge you're attempting to overcome.

Have you ever labelled yourself as a natural optimist or a pessimist? Well, there is one very simple way to dispel the myth that we are either one or the other by simply framing it this way.

We have all had a situation in which we have either found it difficult to go to sleep due to something concerning us or woken up in the early hours of the morning with something on our minds. If we were naturally optimistic then these things would simply not keep us awake.

## Three dimensions of optimism

As I mentioned, optimism is an explanatory style, a dimension that we can move around. It doesn't remain static and it's not about being one (optimistic) or the other (pessimistic). Optimism can be split into three smaller dimensions as a way of explaining how we view the world and life.

+ **Permanence** — how temporary or permanent we see the situation or challenge that we face.
+ **Pervasiveness** — how much or little of our life the challenge impacts.
+ **Personalization** — how much of the challenge is due to our own actions/circumstances or the actions/circumstances of others.

A great way of visually understanding how this is an explanatory style is to try this simple activity which you can do individually or in a group. On the left-hand wall of the room you're now in I want you to visualize the word PESSIMISM written in big letters, and on the right-hand wall written in equally big letters visualize the word OPTIMISM. Now imagine there is a line on the floor stretching between the words from one side of the room to the other, and in the middle is a small cross that signifies neither pessimistic nor optimistic. Now think about a recent challenge or adversity you have faced or may be currently facing and place yourself somewhere along the imaginary line, based on how you view yourself and the challenge from either an optimistic or pessimistic perspective. If you think you're neutral then you'll stand on the cross in the middle. If you're slightly pessimistic about the challenge then you'll stand just to the left of the cross, and the more pessimistic you feel the closer you'll stand to the left-hand wall. The same principle applies if you think you are slightly optimistic about the challenge (stand to the right of the cross) or totally optimistic, in which case you'll stand against the right-hand wall. If you are doing this activity as part of a group there is no need to share your challenge with anyone. Nor will the activity reveal to anyone what the challenge or adversity is that you are thinking about.

Once you are in place somewhere on the line, ask yourself the following questions, which will look at your challenge from the three dimensions of permanence, pervasiveness and personalization — the 3Ps.

## Permanence

Remember that permanence is looking at how temporary or permanent we see the challenge so the question to ask ourselves here is: 'How temporary or permanent is the challenge I'm facing?'

If you believe the challenge is permanent, that it is going to last forever and you will take it to your grave then you would stand alongside the left-hand wall that has 'pessimism' written on it. If you believe the challenge is temporary and going to be over very soon then you would stand alongside the right-hand wall that has 'optimism' written on it. If you believe your challenge is going to be resolved sometime between very soon (temporary) or never (permanent) then you will stand somewhere on the line in between.

Take a moment to see where you are standing on the line and remember that you have put yourself there based on your view from the 'permanence' dimension.

## Pervasiveness

Stay where you are and let's look at the same challenge from a 'pervasiveness' dimension. This dimension looks at how much of our life the challenges impacts. The question to ask yourself is: 'How much or how little does the challenge I'm facing impact my life?'

If you believe the challenge has a lot of influence on your life, then move along the line to stand alongside the left-hand wall where 'pessimism' is written. If you believe the challenge has very little impact on your life, then move along the line to stand alongside the right-hand 'optimism' wall. If your challenge is impacting your life somewhere between a lot to very little then position yourself somewhere on the line in between.

Once you have completed this from a 'pervasiveness' dimension take a moment to have a look at where you are standing and see if you have moved either way along the line from where you were when you looked at the same challenge from the 'permanence' dimension.

## Personalization

Now, staying in the same position along the line, let's again look at the same challenge from the third dimension of 'personalization'. Remember, this is how much of the challenge is due to our actions or circumstances. The question to ask ourselves here is: How much of this challenge is due to your actions or the actions of others?

If you believe the challenge is totally due to your own actions then move along the line to stand alongside the left-hand wall (pessimism); however, if you believe the challenge is totally due to the actions of others then stand alongside the right-hand wall of 'optimism'. Again, if the challenge is between these two extremes move yourself along the line to stand somewhere in between.

Once you're in position, again take a moment to reflect on where you are standing and to see if you have moved from where you were previously when looking at the challenge from a 'pervasiveness' perspective and also from when you looked at the challenge from a 'permanence' perspective. Reflect on where you are standing on the line in relation to the way you responded to the three questions to see if you have moved. Even the slightest of movements between permanence, pervasiveness and personalization dimensions shows us that optimism is actually an explanatory style and, rather than being optimistic or pessimistic, you actually think either more optimistically or more pessimistically depending on which dimension you are looking at in relation to your challenge.

This is a very simple tool to use for any challenges you may face as it recognizes the difference between emotional and explanatory styles. If you can adopt this form of thinking when faced with a challenge, you will build up your resources to have an explanatory style, which reduces potential labelling that you are either a pessimist or an optimist.

By practising this activity, you can start to learn to be more optimistic and therefore add the first tool to your toolkit. We call this the 3P tool.

In our organization, by supporting and empowering people to understand the optimism tool and one of its many uses, we started to see that not only is optimism something we can learn but also that it was having a positive impact upon individuals at work. The language around the office started to change from pessimistic to more positive. Previously I mentioned a staff member whose role was to make sales and bring in revenue to the organization. He had failed to meet a deadline to produce a sales report by which we could analyse our financial data. He then claimed there was no point in following people up for a potential sale as they were going to say no anyway. After learning and practising his optimism skills and looking at his challenges with his 3P tool, we saw a complete change in language that looked something like the tables on the next three pages.

Challenging 'permanence': Making sales calls and confirming orders

| Explanatory style | Thinking pattern | Example |
|---|---|---|
| Pessimistic | Bad events are permanent | 'I'm never going to get that sale so I won't bother making that phone call.' |
| Pessimistic | Good events are temporary | 'I got some great sales the other day but who knows when I'll get the next one?' |
| Optimistic | Bad events are temporary | 'I didn't get any sales today but I'm sure I'll get some better results tomorrow.' |
| Optimistic | Good events are permanent | 'I enjoy my job and I can see the difference my sales make to the company.' |

Challenging 'pervasiveness': Writing a report to pitch for a new client

| Explanatory style | Thinking pattern | Example |
| --- | --- | --- |
| Pessimistic | Bad events are universal | 'I'm not confident in my job in any way whatsoever.' |
| Pessimistic | Good events are specific | 'I'm only good at the report writing part of my job, nothing else.' |
| Optimistic | Bad events are specific | 'I struggle with the report writing part of my job.' |
| Optimistic | Good events are universal | 'I'm good at my job; this will be a great report.' |

Challenging 'personalization': Meeting a deadline

| Explanatory style | Thinking pattern | Example |
|---|---|---|
| Pessimistic | Attribute bad events to yourself | 'I'm hopeless at my work, I knew I would let them down.' |
| Pessimistic | Credit other people/ circumstances for good events | 'If it wasn't for Jane, we wouldn't have made it.' |
| Optimistic | Attribute bad events to other people/ circumstances | 'It was impossible to do that in the time they set for me.' |
| Optimistic | Credit yourself for good events | 'It was my effective organization that helped us finish the task on time.' |

# The ABCDE tool

Another tool that will support you in building optimistic thoughts when facing challenges is called the ABCDE tool.

+ A = Activating event
+ B = Beliefs or thoughts about that event
+ C= Consequences
+ D = Dispute or Distraction
+ E = Energize

To explain, let's look at a scenario that at some point we have all been through.

## ABC

Imagine you are at work and you receive an email first thing in the morning — this is the *activating event*. The email states that you have to attend a staff meeting at 2 p.m. that afternoon. Now imagine that when you received the email you thought to yourself, 'Oh, great. Another useless staff meeting called at the last minute, which will again be a waste of time. Don't these people know how much work I've got to do?' These are your *beliefs or thoughts about the event*. In this scenario, what do you think might be the consequences of such beliefs or thoughts?

More than likely you would have been not overly happy when you attended the meeting, were possibly distracted thinking about the work you had to do and not prepared to contribute actively, etc. The *consequences* of this could be that your body language screams out to others that you're not interested, you may feel more stressed and anxious or you might simply become less engaged with your workplace.

Now let's imagine that when receiving the same email (activating event) you thought to yourself (beliefs or thoughts), 'Great! A staff meeting. I wonder what I'll hear about today and learn. Also, I might get the opportunity to catch up with Sara and lock in some time to look at that project we were talking about.' In this case, it's more than likely you would have attended the meeting feeling happy, looking forward to what you might learn and thinking of ways to contribute. The consequences of this could be that you feel energized or excited, engaged with what you are doing and generally positive about the opportunities that might come from this.

As we can see in both examples, the activating event was the same yet the beliefs or thoughts about the event changed the consequences. So the question to ask ourselves here is: do we have the ability to change our beliefs or thoughts and if so, how do we do this? When we are aware that our B (beliefs) are not very helpful and may lead to unhelpful C (consequences), then we need to use the letter D (dispute or distraction) to change the B.

## Disputing

*Disputing* is looking at the evidence for your belief and being able to adjust your thoughts if there is reasonable evidence to show that your original belief is wrong.

I used to believe that I was not and could never be a good handyman. If there were any small jobs that needed doing around the house, such as hanging up pictures on the wall or fixing up the side gate properly to stop the dog escaping, I would usually avoid doing them or believe that putting a cardboard box in front of the hole in the gate would be good enough to stop the dog from getting out until it rained and the box got wet and disintegrated. My emotional thoughts generally took over and I would often say to myself that I simply didn't have the skill to do a good job so I'd be better off not doing anything. Statements would roll around my head such as, 'If I try to drill a hole in the wall I'll probably make it too big to hang the picture up, and then I'll have to fix the wall.'

However, once I became open to disputing my original thoughts I was able to actually challenge my thinking based on the evidence in front of me. For a start, I had never really tried to learn how to do these jobs properly, nor did I have the appropriate tools (screwdrivers, a drill, etc.) required to enable me to fix the problems. So by taking myself to my local hardware store I was able to seek advice from an expert, who provided me with both the information and equipment I needed to fix the side gate and hang up the pictures. By following the instructions given to me and utilizing the tools I had just bought I was able to tackle both jobs. I'm not saying it was instant success, and at times I wanted to give up with frustration, but I persevered and finally completed the job.

By disputing my thoughts — that I was no good at doing handyman jobs around the house — and showing that there was no real evidence to support my belief, I was able to free my mind and take on a different belief and in turn build my personal resources. I know that I will never be the world's best handyman but I now have the confidence to tackle such challenges at home as well as the evidence to back me up, as the dog no longer escapes and the pictures haven't fallen off the wall. So if I could do it once, there is nothing stopping me being able to do it multiple times with simply a bit more practice.

A good question to ask yourself when looking to change your B is: 'What evidence do I have that supports my original belief?'

## Distraction

The tool of disputing is another way of creating an explanatory style that supports a more optimistic thinking pattern and allows us to analyse the evidence for the belief we have and adjust that belief if there is reasonable evidence it is wrong. This tool is, however, very difficult to use when you are experiencing intense emotions, and if this is the case then the *distraction* tool is a better option as it allows you to potentially avoid any unhelpful behaviour until you can think more clearly.

A good example of this happened one day at work when I found myself facilitating a meeting between two of my managers who simply couldn't agree on the direction required and resources needed to map out a project they were working on. Their inability to reach an agreement was fuelled by each of them experiencing intense emotions at times, which were a reaction to something the other said. This in turn had impacted each of their teams, who also were getting frustrated with the lack of progress and uncertainty over what would happen and how, which in turn created even more pressure for both managers. In cases such as this, when emotions run high and distort our ability to think clearly, we can aim to distract ourselves.

During our meeting the roadblocks that each manager thought the other was putting up quickly surfaced and the blame game started. With this, emotions and tensions became raised, and arguments and counter arguments began. The conversation started to become personal and frustrating.

In order to create a circuit breaker, a distraction had to occur. The meeting was called to a temporary halt and I suggested the three of us go for a walk outside. The fresh air, sunshine and change of scenery would at the very least do us all some good. Despite some initial uncertainties both agreed. The first few minutes were filled with a stony silence as we walked one behind the other down the footpath. However, after a while we got distracted by something in the street, which led to one of us talking about something that had happened on the weekend. This then carried us on for a few minutes, with all three of us contributing to the conversation. We even had the occasional laugh. At some point during the walk I was able to say, 'Hey Craig, you know that Lucy does care about the project and its overall success for the organization.' After a little hesitation we were then able to discuss and calmly dispute some of their thoughts on how the situation had got to where it was. We established that both of them were passionate about working for the organization and that success relied on us working together. This then led us to discuss and agree that the two of them needed to work together. Some acknowledgements were also made that they had both been feeling under pressure and rushed in their approach to work, so we agreed to look at how we could put some measures in place to support both of them and prevent this situation happening again.

By the time we got back to the office the mood had completely changed and both managers were prepared to continue the meeting and be open to working towards solutions. We had been able to distract ourselves from an unhelpful emotional position and use the dispute tool to analyse the evidence for the beliefs or thoughts that were hindering us, then adjust that belief based on the reasonable evidence that we worked through.

We were fortunate enough to be able to resolve the challenge fairly quickly by first using our distraction tool before moving on to the dispute tool. However, it's important to note that some situations may not be as quickly resolved as this one, depending on how much emotion has been invested. If the emotion is so high and intense that there is very little chance that disputing may help, then at the very least distracting yourself from the current situation or thought can avoid any further unhelpful behaviour until such time that you are able to think more clearly about it and not exacerbate the problem. There are some exceptional circumstances when it's not appropriate to change your belief to the adversity you face as it will not change the consequences. Such circumstances can be so severe that your emotions are driven by the circumstance itself, not the beliefs about the circumstance. When a loved one dies, the emotions that follow largely stem from the exceptional circumstance and tragedy itself, not from your interpretation of the circumstances. This does not mean that one's beliefs play no role in healing from the tragedy and that the ABCDE tool serves no purpose. In fact, your beliefs and resilience determine how quickly and how easily you will regain control of your emotions and behaviours and therefore bounce back.

## Energize

The energize step involves simply aiming to pay attention to how you feel when you have successfully disputed a negative thought. Do you feel less anxious, lighter, a sense of liveliness, stronger in spirit, etc.? If so, then acknowledge these feelings and reinforce this by writing a few sentences about how your distraction has changed the way you feel. For example, what has happened to your mood, what behaviour has changed, are you more open to possibilities and did you find a solution that you couldn't see before? By doing this you reinforce a good skill set that you are learning while at the same time broadening your resources.

---

This chapter has looked at what optimism is — a tendency to expect the best possible outcome or dwell on the most hopeful aspects of a situation — and how having some can broaden our thinking and build our personal resources. It's about being able to see the path you are on and the rocks in front of you that may block the way, yet also seeing a way to navigate yourself around those blocks. Many studies have shown the that having regular positive emotions in your life leads to greater health and longevity. One such study evaluated the optimistic quality of entrance letters of young girls entering a convent to become nuns. Their living conditions were all the same, including diet, tasks, lifestyle and environment. The women were followed over their lifespan and the more optimistic women lived, on average, more than twelve years longer than their more pessimistic counterparts.[1]

With the above in mind you might like to take five minutes to complete the following Optimism Inventory. Answer the questions to see how you score and how the key points listed at the end of this chapter can support you in building a more optimistic explanatory style.

### Optimism Inventory

The purpose of this short questionnaire is to provide you with an opportunity to gain an insight into how optimism might be playing out for you. While the questionnaire is built with best-practice frameworks, it is not designed to be a valid scientific reflection. Take care in the way you review your results; they are best used as a conversation piece to explore positive actions that can be taken to further orient yourself towards a more positive and flourishing approach to your personal and/or professional life.

Below are seven statements. Read each statement and then ask yourself: 'To what degree is this statement like me?' Use the following scale to indicate how much like you each statement is:

+ Definitely not like me = 1 point
+ Not much like me = 2 points
+ Not really sure = 3 points
+ Somewhat like me = 4 points
+ Definitely like me = 5 points

| Statement | Score |
|---|---|
| 1. I never get disheartened when things don't go as planned. Everything always works out for the best. | |
| 2. There is always a solution to every problem and I never give up until I find it. | |
| 3. I always find it easy to see the bright side of every situation. | |
| 4. Even when things are clearly not working out, I always believe everything will be fine. | |
| 5. I get frustrated easily with people who say something 'can't be done'. | |
| 6. It doesn't matter how bad things get — every cloud has a silver lining. | |
| 7. If something goes wrong and I know I have tried my best, I don't blame myself. | |
| Total | |

Insights to consider

Now tally up your score from the questionnaire.

## Higher score (25–35)

A score in this bracket indicates you probably tend to see the best in most situations. This may assist you with finding solutions and solving problems. You may also generally recover reasonably quickly from setbacks and help others do the same. Watch for times when you may become impatient with others who appear to be negative, or when you don't give others enough time to recover.

## Mid-range score (16–24)

You might find there are some situations in which you are more optimistic than others. This might not always make sense to you and you may be perplexed as to the difference. It is worth reflecting upon when it is easier or harder to be optimistic so you can adjust where required.

## Lower score (5–15)

You might find it difficult to recover quickly from some setbacks. You may get easily frustrated when things don't go well and tend to give up or hand something over to others to do. You may also get frustrated when others don't listen to your concerns when you put them forward. Watch if you tend to put forward negative views too quickly at times.

# To sum up

The key points and tools from this chapter for our ORANGES toolkit are:

+ Optimism is something that can be learned and practised.
+ Developing a more optimistic explanatory style to challenges can be more helpful.
+ Optimism and pessimism are dimensions you can move around on, and can be split into three smaller dimensions.
+ You can apply the 3Ps tool (permanence, pervasiveness and personalization) to show that you are not always optimistic or always pessimistic.
+ The ABCDE tool can be used to help make your explanatory style more optimistic.
+ Emotions can influence how we think, and in times of heightened emotion Distraction may work better that Disputation.
+ If you practise using the 3Ps and ABCDE tools, you should be able to enhance your positive emotions and have the capacity to broaden your thinking and build your personal resources.

# 2

# Resilience

**Resilience** (*noun*) The capacity to withstand and adapt to the challenges life throws at us.

> The greatest glory in living lies not in never falling, but in rising every time we fall.
>
> **Nelson Mandela**

Resilience is the power and ability to recover; it's a form of buoyancy and bounce-back. It's a skill that anyone can learn to not only survive but thrive. Resilience is a crucial factor to a happy and healthy life. More than anything else it's what determines how we tackle the setbacks, adversity and challenges that come our way and how quickly it takes for us to rise above these. From losing a loved one to the impact of a natural disaster, everyone has resilience and it's not just an innate ability — it's something that can be built on and learned.

Former Australian Prime Minister Malcolm Fraser once said, 'life was not meant to be easy' and, to be frank, life has a tendency to throw its fair share of disappointments our way. Some people seem to have more resilience than others, but the truth is that everyone is born with a certain level of resilience. It's just that some people are more skilled at actively applying resilience and regulating their emotions than others, which allows them to draw on what they know when they need it most. In our lives we all know or come across resilient people, whether they are public figures such as Nelson Mandela or closer to home, perhaps a family member, friend or work colleague. They inspire us and seem to excel in spite of the challenges in their lives. They are able to fulfil their potential despite, or even because of, adversity and tend to see challenges as opportunities for growth and renewal. In fact, the most resilient people seek new experiences because they know it's only through challenging and pushing themselves to their limits that they will broaden their thinking and build their personal resources.

Resilient people acknowledge that failures happen and that these failures won't define them for the rest of their lives. They don't hold on to disappointment when they don't succeed; they use the knowledge of failure as a springboard to bounce forward and move further than they otherwise would. Resilience also enables you to achieve at the highest level, to have fulfilling relationships, maintain energy and to be healthy and happy. I don't want to paint a picture here that resilient people are superhuman, as they have the same doubts, disappointments, fears and anxieties as most people. However, they have learned how to stop these from overwhelming them.

We all have spikes in our levels of happiness when good and bad things happen to us. If we were to draw a line graph to represent the happiness in our life it may look something like the graph below.

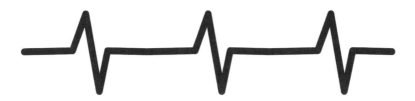

Those peaks and troughs might look something like this: left school, got a job, didn't get a promotion, travelled overseas, got another job, brought a car, broke up with partner, my sporting team won the championship, got married, was made redundant, lost someone close to me, had my first child, etc.

The horizontal line in the graph represents the happiness or emotional set point that everyone has. Some people's happiness set point may be higher or lower than others, and everyone's set point is different depending on the level of resilience you are born with. As we go through life, positive and negative things happen to us; they can be both minor and major on both the positive and negative ledgers, but the point is we all have a basic level of happiness.

Everyone is born with a certain set point for happiness in the same way we are born with a certain set point for weight. Some of us are more fortunate to possess genes that allow us to keep a steady weight without really trying, while others have to constantly work hard at maintaining their weight by watching what they eat.

When positive events occur we experience a spike in our levels of happiness: buying our first apartment or car, getting a pay rise or having a holiday. Can you recall that feeling of excitement and anticipation when you were about to go on a holiday? All the planning and research you've done to secure the best deal and have everything organized. The joy you felt when you left work that last afternoon, knowing that you were now officially on holiday, the euphoria and excitement when you arrived at your destination, how relaxed you felt and how time seemed to fly by. Recall, too, that feeling when the holiday is over, you're back at work and back into the normal routine of life — the excitement of the holiday seems to wear off and we revert to our original happiness set point.

We also have dips in our happiness when we experience negative events or adversity in our life. I can remember the feeling of great sadness when I broke up with my first girlfriend. At the time I felt the pain of rejection and that life had dealt me a heavy blow; I was sure she was the only girl for me and that there would never be another person like her in my life. However, after a period of time my life reverted back to its normal routine. I started to realize that the negative thoughts telling me there wouldn't be anyone else out there for me were not correct and I started to socialize again, meet other people, lose the pain of that first break-up and revert to my normal happiness set point.

We all have ups and downs in our lives, and while we adapt to those positives and negatives some people adapt faster and have greater resilience than others. However, at some point we all return to our happiness set point. And by learning certain skills and techniques we can, over time, increase our happiness set point and therefore increase the duration and intensity of our positive experiences, as well as decrease the impact of our negative experiences.

# The Four As of emotional management and resilience

The major roadblock to building resilience is not our genetics, our upbringing, the type of job we do or how much wealth we have. It's how we look at and think about the situation we are in or facing. Using the tools outlined in Chapter 1, such as the ABCDE tool, to build optimism will also support the building of resilience.

In their book *The Resilience Factor*, Karen Reivich and Andrew Shatte outlined how resilience can also be practised through a number of strategies that help us manage our emotions or dispute negative thoughts. They also reveal how neurology shows us that our emotions, brain and body are intricately linked and how we can change the way we feel by adjusting how we think or hold our body. We know that positive emotions improve our immune system and calm us after a negative experience, they make us healthier, help us live longer, make us more tolerant to pain, help us recover quicker from illness and be more socially engaged. They allow our brain to function well, providing it with the fuel we need to think clearly and relax. The more laughter, love and good emotions we experience and share with family, friends, neighbours and work colleagues, the more we expand our ability to shift negative emotions and bounce back.[1]

American scholar and researcher Professor Dr Brené Brown, who spent over a decade studying emotions, states: 'If we don't allow ourselves to experience joy and love, we will definitely miss out on filling our reservoir with what we need when hard things happen.'[2]

Author and seasoned resilience coach Karen Reivich says the following:

Your thinking style is a lens through which we view the world. Everyone has such a lens and it colours the way we interpret the events in our lives. Your thinking style is what causes you to respond emotionally to events, so it's your level of resilience — your ability to overcome, steer through and bounce back when adversity occurs.[3]

Resilience is built on the knowledge that our emotions and behaviours are triggered not by events themselves but how we interpret those events. A good tool to help us in this regard is called the Four As of emotional management and resilience. By using this tool, you can learn to improve the management of your emotions and therefore become more resilient. The Four As are:

+ awareness
+ acceptance
+ adjustment
+ action.

*Awareness* involves being aware of the emotions you are experiencing and what is going on in your body and brain. Without awareness you can't do much to change these things. Emotions contain information that can support you in figuring out how to help yourself. For example, you can ask yourself: 'What am I feeling, where is the tension, and what is this telling me about myself and the situation I'm in?' Such questions will help increase your awareness of your emotions and your physical response to a situation.

*Acceptance* is about acknowledging that it's perfectly fine to be feeling the way you are. Emotions are a natural response to the experiences we encounter. There are no good or bad emotions — they are all there for a reason. If you start judging yourself by saying, for example, 'I shouldn't be feeling angry' or 'I shouldn't be feeling ecstatic' then what emotion does that judgment conjure up? More often it will add an emotion of guilt and a feeling that you have done something wrong or failed in an obligation. Also, by not acknowledging or skipping acceptance of your emotions, you can increase your guilt and your strategies to help yourself won't work. Accepting the situation you're in, accepting your emotional response to it and what you can and can't control within that situation, is a big part of building resilience.

The crucial question to ask yourself in these situations is: 'Is this emotion serving me well right now for the space I'm in?' If your answer is yes, then feel free to stay within that emotion. Sometimes people may choose to stay where they are and be immersed in their emotion — if it's a conscious decision to do this, then maybe that's okay. However, if your answer is no then you need to adjust.

*Adjustment* comes about only when we have acknowledged acceptance and are prepared to make some choices. At this point we can ask ourselves: 'What adjustments can I make to improve the situation I'm in? How can I shift my thinking, my energy and my body? What negative self-talk have I been repeating to myself that has contributed to this situation, and what positive beliefs and thinking can I start to put into place that are more helpful and accurate right now?'

*Action* involves consciously and intelligently making a change. By using your emotional awareness, you can look back on the last time you were in a state of indecisiveness and remember the feeling you had when you decided to make a change and took action. What positive changes happened as a result?

## Strategies to change your emotions

The strategies we have in our toolkit to help us change the emotion we are currently feeling generally fall into four categories:

+ brain-based strategies — activities that change the way we are thinking

+ body-based strategies — activities that change our physiology
+ environmental-based strategies — activities that change our environment
+ relationship-based strategies — activities that involve others.

Imagine it's the end of a very busy and challenging week. You've had several tight deadlines to meet at work, which has meant you've put in some long hours. You've had to juggle and renegotiate some social and domestic commitments that your family wanted you to attend, and being coach of the local basketball side you've had to organize and manage the training of a group of twelve-year-olds. With little time for much else and not a great deal of sleep, domestic chores such as cleaning and doing the laundry have piled up, the food shopping hasn't been done and the fridge is looking pretty empty. The thought of coming home at the end of a challenging week, already feeling tired, to an untidy house with no food is not the most appealing.

With the above scenario in mind, look at the table on the next page and write in each square the activities you currently do to improve your state of mind and mood from a brain, body, environment and relationship perspective. For example, for the brain you might listen to some relaxing music, for the body you may have a soak in a nice hot bath, for the environment you might decide to go out for dinner and for relationships you might talk to a friend or your partner. When writing down your activities it's okay to find that some of these may sit across a number of different strategies. For example, going to the movies could be an activity you write down as both an environmental and relationship strategy.

To help you get started here are some suggested activities you might use after a busy week at work. See if you agree with these or add other activities to create your own list.

**Brain**

Listen to music — relax your mind

Play video games — distract yourself with something you enjoy and feel energized by

Meditate — develop a mindfulness practice

Talk with friends — talk about things that lift your mood

**Body**

Have a hot bath/shower — relax your body

Go to the gym — energize yourself with exercise

Sleep — help your body recover and recharge

Do yoga — stretch your body and control your breathing

Eat a healthy meal — provide fuel for your body

**Environment**

Go out for dinner — change your environment to shift your emotion

Tidy up — create a fresh new space

Go away for the weekend — new places to see and things to do

Do some gardening — sense of achievement and helping the garden flourish

**Relationships**

Talk to friends — connect with like-minded people

Smile and make others feel good — create a connection

Go out for dinner with someone — build on your friendship and/or relationship

Buy and give a gift to someone — create surprise and gratitude

The purpose of this is to show that we already have a number and range of strategies in our toolkit and that they can be used over a number of situations as it's not a one-size-fits-all approach. It's important to have a range of strategies to be able to handle a range of situations. For example, imagine that the only strategy I use to help me relax is to exercise at the gym. If, however, I unfortunately sustain a back strain and can't go to the gym then I'm likely to feel more frustrated about the situation. But if I have other relaxation strategies in my toolkit I could use these while recovering from my back strain. For example, I might go and have a massage, or meet up with a friend for coffee, play a video game or go to the movies.

Over the years I've had one particular situation in which I have used the Four As tool on a regular basis to good effect. Many years ago, my mother was diagnosed with the early signs of Alzheimer's disease just before my father passed away. They had been together for more than five decades and my father's passing increased the impact of Mum's diagnosis. The emotions I experienced at the time both in my body and brain were raw, tense, unsettling, fearful and confusing as I watched my mother — who had been an active, intelligent and self-made woman — spiral into a rapid decline of impaired thinking, memory loss and physical inactivity. These emotions were impacting my normal day-to-day ability to function clearly, as I juggled trying to manage the care of my mother with maintaining the activities and challenges of normal everyday family and work life.

Many of my go-to strategies, such as going to the gym to clear my brain, feel fitter and to get some time to myself, were thrown out the window as I felt the pressure of being busy and overwhelmed. However, I failed to substitute going to the gym with something else that would provide similar relief, such as taking the dog for a walk or going for a bike ride with the kids. In other words, I relied too heavily on using the same strategies, rather than having a mixture of strategies at my disposal that I could easily use to the same effect if one of them wasn't available.

By asking myself the question, 'Is this emotion serving me well right now for the space I'm in?' I was able to accept that the frustrations and anger I felt for my mother's situation were absolutely okay. It was quite alright for me to feel that my mother had been dealt a poor hand with this disease and that life would not turn out the way she had wanted it to be. However, I also became conscious that staying in these emotions for the long term was not going to help my mother, myself or my family in making the progress we all needed to ensure she received the right care and support. Coming to this point allowed me to be proactive and make the necessary adjustments to accept my emotions (good or bad) and look for new strategies to improve the situation. Once I was happy with the thought and planning of these new strategies I could then action and put them into place.

Ultimately the Four As tool allowed me to deal with a confronting and long-term challenge and in time become comfortable with it, and to look for the positives with great purpose and action.

Now that you understand you can have a range of strategies for a range of emotions that you may experience, it's important to acknowledge that some of those strategies will either be sustainable or unstainable depending on the situation you find ourselves in. For example, a sustainable strategy for you to relax after a hard day at work might be to have a glass of wine; however, if you have a whole bottle of wine each day after work then this strategy will be obviously unsustainable. You may want to take some time to reflect on your strategies to ensure those that might impact your health are used in moderation and that you can switch them on and off when needed.

# Thinking traps

Another skill to help sustain resilience is to avoid what Karen Reivich and Andrew Shatte, authors of *The Resilience Factor*, describe as 'thinking traps'. Our thinking style is the key to building resilience and as we are prone to make mistakes we have at some stage in our lives all made 'thinking trap' errors. Usually it is more common that we tend to be consistently vulnerable to two or three of these traps, rather than every one of them all the time.

Some typical thinking traps include the following:

+ **Jumping to conclusions**. This involves making assumptions without the relevant data. People who operate in this space tend to do things quickly or make snap responses. If you find yourself engaging in this kind of thinking, try slowing down by thinking about what you are saying before you say it or by taking a few deep breathes to slow down your breathing and refocus your mind. Then ask yourself what evidence you are basing your conclusion on and if you have all the facts at your disposal to make the right conclusion.

+ **Tunnel vision**. A tendency to focus exclusively on a single or limited objective or view characterizes tunnel vision. When operating in this space, a good tool to help move you from a narrow to a broader view is to write down your view on one side of a piece of paper, then ask yourself, 'What is the big picture here?' and write down your answer on the other side. Then, ask yourself and write down as many responses to the following questions: 'How important is this one aspect to the big picture?', 'What is a fair assessment of the entire situation?', 'Is it possible that there may be other alternatives?' By answering these questions and writing down the responses you will train your brain to broaden your thinking beyond only having a narrow view.

+ **Magnifying and minimizing.** People who magnify the negative and minimize the positive are often not aware that they are in a thinking trap. If this is you, then at the end of the day write down the positive things you did or the things you did well that day. It doesn't matter how small or insignificant you may think they are, write them down and acknowledge that they happened. By the end of the week you will have started to build a portfolio of evidence to show that good things happen to you and therefore create a more balanced view. Resilience rests on an accurate appraisal of one's life. Extreme pessimists and extreme optimists will suffer equally.

+ **Personalizing.** This is the tendency to attribute problems to your own doing. If you operate like this, try to ask yourself these questions: 'Did anyone or anything else contribute to the situation?', 'How much of the problem is due to me and how much is due to others?'

+ **Externalizing.** The opposite to personalizing, this thinking trap involves the tendency to reject that problems are your own doing. If this is you then you need to start holding yourself accountable by asking yourself: 'What else might I have done to create a different situation?', 'What did I really do to contribute to the current situation, and was it helpful?', 'How much of the situation is due to me, and how much is due to others?'

+ **Overgeneralizing.** When we engage in this kind of thinking, we generalize beyond appropriate or justified limits. If you do this then you need to ask yourself why, for what purpose and what are your behaviours that stem from this? By looking at the situation and deliberately narrowing your explanation, you can get closer to a more logical and accurate explanation that will then modify your behaviour. There will then be less chance that people will doubt your character.

+ **Mind reading**. This involves the tendency to believe that we know what others are thinking and we act accordingly. People who fall in to this thinking trap need to ensure that they speak up, ask questions of others and seek to understand before they themselves are understood. Ask yourself: 'Have I communicated all of the relevant information clearly?', 'Have I made my feelings and beliefs known?', 'Am I expecting the other person to figure out my needs?'

+ **Emotional reasoning**. This occurs if you usually draw false conclusions about things based on your emotional state. In this case, you need to separate your feelings from the facts. Write down as many facts as possible about the emotional situation you face and then ask yourself if your feelings accurately reflect the facts of that situation. If you don't know the facts, then try to find out what questions you must ask to know the facts.[4]

# Grit

Some further research by American psychologist Professor Angela Duckworth has shown that having grit can also enhance our levels of resilience. Duckworth describes grit as the perseverance and passion for long-term goals, and although she doesn't diminish the importance of short-term or immediate goals, Duckworth's research is conducted in the context of achieving excellence in performance.[5]

So what is grit? It's certainly not about how talented or lucky you are, but more about how driven you are to achieve something.

It's something you care much about and it gives meaning to almost everything you do. Grit is the glue that keeps you focused even when obstacles are put in your way and slow you down, or when things don't work out the way you anticipate. Your talent and luck play a part in your success but they alone don't guarantee that you will have tenacity that grit requires.

The five main characteristics of grit are:

+ Courage: Your ability to manage fear of failure is strong and gritty people are not afraid to fail but instead use failure as a learning curve to improve themselves.
+ Conscientiousness: You have an ability to plan and be meticulous in detail.
+ Long-term goals: You have a vision for something that requires a long-term commitment and you are prepared to work to make it happen.
+ Optimism and confidence: You have an ability to believe in your goal no matter what may derail you and the self-assurance to keep at it.
+ Excellence: In general, gritty people don't seek perfection but instead strive for excellence.[6]

In reading the above you might think the characteristics outlined by Duckworth really only relate to high-performance athletes or business people. But the reality is they are the characteristics that everyday people draw upon as well. For example, some friends of mine recently decided to have a change in life. They packed in their city jobs and moved to the country where they bought a bed-and-breakfast business in which they needed to use all the characteristics of grit to help them succeed.

They used courage to leave the safety of their city lifestyle and work to take on a whole new lifestyle in the country without a regular income. They needed to prepare themselves for failure and in certain areas they did but they used these as a springboard for growth and development. They worked on a plan as to what they wanted their business to be known for and mapped out how they were going to achieve this. They constantly reviewed what they were doing and sought feedback from others who were more skilled than they were. They worked hard and put in the hours to ensure their goal had every chance of success. An optimistic outlook helped them believe they could in time overcome the obstacles that would get in their way, such as limited resources and knowledge. And finally, they never sought perfection but certainly looked for excellence even in the smallest things, and this is what they now have become known for within their business

So whether you are someone who likes restoring old cars in your garage, are determined to graduate from university or aiming to complete your first marathon, grit on its own may not be sufficient for success but it sure is necessary.

---

This chapter has looked at what resilience is — the capacity to withstand and adapt to the challenges life throws at us — and how it is a crucial ingredient to having a happy and healthy life. It's not just an ability we are born with and need to survive; it's a skill that we can learn, improve on and in turn draw on to thrive. Resilience comes when you believe that you have the power to control the things in your life and have the ability and accurate belief to change what needs changing. Practising the above skills will result in improvement in how you communicate, make decisions and generally deal with life's challenges by recognizing and changing negative thoughts, self-talk and beliefs that are subconsciously undermining your resilience.

One study found that individuals who coped with the stress of the September 11 attacks in the United States used positive emotions in the aftermath of a crisis to buffer themselves against depression, which in turn helped them to thrive.[7] By broadening our thinking we can build our personal resilience resources, and this can bolster our levels of optimism, prepare us to take more chances and help us embrace our lives.

You might now like to take five minutes to complete the following Resilience Inventory by answering a number of multiple choice questions to see how you score and how the key points listed at the end of this chapter can support you in building a more resilient thinking style.

### Resilience Inventory

The purpose of this short questionnaire is to provide you with an opportunity to gain an insight into how resilience might be playing out for you. While the questionnaire is built with best-practice frameworks, it is not designed to be a valid scientific reflection.

Take care in the way you review your results; they are best used as a conversation piece to explore positive actions that can be taken to further orient yourself towards a more positive and flourishing approach to your personal and/or professional life.

Below are seven statements. Read each statement and then ask yourself: 'To what degree is this statement like me?' Use the following scale to indicate how much like you each statement is:

+ Definitely not like me    = 1 point
+ Not much like me          = 2 points
+ Not really sure           = 3 points
+ Somewhat like me          = 4 points
+ Definitely like me        = 5 points

| Statement | Score |
|---|---|
| 1. It never takes me long to recover from setbacks and get back on track with things. | |
| 2. I accept that things don't always work out and find a way to keep going. | |
| 3. I get frustrated with others who give up too easily and take a long time to recover from setbacks. | |
| 4. When faced with a setback I can usually find a new perspective through which to view the problem. | |
| 5. I look at challenges as a way to learn and improve. | |
| 6. I usually come up with the right solution when faced with challenges. | |
| 7. If something I try doesn't work the first time, I am always ready to try something else. | |
| Total | |

Now tally up your score from the questionnaire.

## Higher score (25–35)

If your score falls within this range, you probably tend to be able to recover reasonably quickly from setbacks and get on with things. You may be able to see things from various viewpoints, enabling you to accept setbacks quicker and find productive ways forward. Watch out for times when you refuse to give up and potentially put yourself at risk of burn-out.

## Mid-range score (16–24)

You may find there are some situations where you are more resilient than others. This might not always make sense to you and you might be perplexed as to the difference. It is worth reflecting upon when your levels of resilience change so you can be prepared for unexpected challenges.

## Lower score (5–15)

You might find it difficult to recover quickly from some setbacks and find yourself procrastinating. You may also find that it is difficult to get motivated when you have been disappointed or let down. You may also find that you doubt yourself and don't share ideas, or take action even when you have a good idea.

# To sum up

The key points and tools from this chapter for our ORANGES toolkit are:

+ Resilience is the capacity to withstand and adapt to the challenges life throws at us.
+ Resilience can be learned.
+ We all have a natural happiness set point.
+ The Four As (awareness, acceptance, adjustment, action) provide a simple process to remember and follow. Using these on a regular basis can help broaden your thinking and build your personal resources.
+ Remember the importance of acceptance. You can't move on to change an emotion until there has been an acceptance of the emotion you are in.
+ Ask the question, 'Is this emotion serving me well for the space I'm in?' If not, then change it.
+ Write down your strategies for helping you change emotions, based on the different dimensions of body, brain, environment and relationships.
+ Having a range of strategies is important to apply to different emotions.
+ Try to add a strategy from a different dimension now and again to expand your repertoire.
+ Consider whether your strategies are sustainable or unsustainable.
+ Avoid thinking traps.
+ Your thinking style is the key to boosting resilience.
+ Grit on its own may not be sufficient for success but it sure is necessary.

# 3

## Attitude

**Attitude** (*noun*) A feeling or opinion about something or someone, or a way of behaving that is caused by this.

> Attitude is a little thing that makes a big difference.
>
> **Winston Churchill**

Attitude is something we bring to every situation. It is one of the few human freedoms that can't be taken away from you, as you and you alone can control it — we maintain our ability to choose ours attitude in any given circumstance. This is clearly born out in

Viktor Frankl's book *Man's Search for Meaning*, which chronicles Viktor's own experiences as a prisoner of Auschwitz during World War II. Viktor's story is an example of how a man can have every liberty taken away from him except his ability to choose his own attitude.[1]

From the moment we wake up in the morning to when we go to bed at night, there are always choices to make. Every day and every hour we are offered opportunities to make decisions that determine our behaviours. This not only influences the way we behave but the impact we will have on ourselves and others around us. There are a number of tools we can use that will support our ability to broaden our thinking and build our personal resources around our attitude. The better we understand what influences our attitude and what tools to use, the more choice we have in our actions.

## Understanding behaviours: the iceberg

To unpack attitude we need to understand what behaviours are, and that there are two elements to why we behave the way we do in particular situations or under certain conditions. In essence, behaviours are demonstrated actions, the things that we can see and/or hear. And we have a choice over what these actions will be.

Everyone experiences times when their emotions seem too intense for the situation they are facing or when their behaviour has been over the top or out of line. Have you ever felt deeply guilty about something that normally would have affected you in a moderate way, or have you been ecstatic over something that normally you would feel merely pleased about? Or have you ever been surprised by the extent to which an emotion has led to you behave in a way that is not normally you, for example letting off steam by being aggressive to someone in a traffic jam even though it's not their fault?

These situations show that there are deeper influences at play that revolve around our strongly held beliefs, values and motivations, and which in many cases we have learned from our parents or families. These are the beliefs we have learned from a young age and been reinforced to us over a period of time, a learned view rather than an inherent view of the world and our place within it. These beliefs are deep within our consciousness and often outside of our day-to-day awareness, and since this is the case we need to use a special tool to detect them: an iceberg.

Imagine you're on a boat in the Southern Ocean near the Antarctic, looking at a huge iceberg. From your position, how much of the iceberg can you see? Although the iceberg is big, the reality is that what we see floating on top of the water represents only about 10 per cent of the total iceberg, with the remaining 90 per cent sitting under the water and out of view. By using this analogy it's not too dissimilar to looking at our own lives — much of what we show to the outside world is only about 10 per cent with the other 90 per cent sitting below the surface.

The diagram on the next page represents our lives, showing some visible or more obvious influences above the water line. Now ask yourself what the influences are in your own life that others cannot see, that sit below the surface yet influence your behaviours, and perhaps write these down. I've given you a head start with a few examples in the illustration, so see if you can add to this list.

If we want to know what makes people behave in a certain way and why, then we need to understand what lies deep beneath the surface for them. The only way of doing this is by getting to know the beliefs and values that lie beneath the surface of their iceberg. The same goes for better understanding ourselves. Most of the differences or personality clashes that occur in our lives, whether they are with our partner, family members, work colleagues, neighbours or even people we don't know, are due to differences in iceberg beliefs.

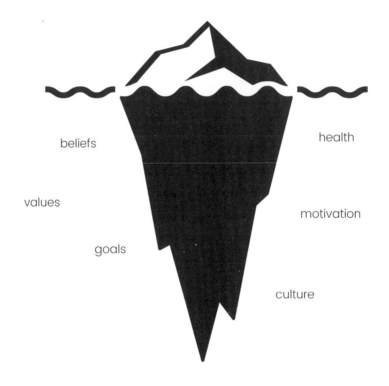

beliefs

health

values

motivation

goals

culture

## Emotion

When looking at all the words you have written under the surface in your iceberg to outline what drives your behaviour, there is one key word that is important for us to consider further — emotion. In many cases it's not the values, self-esteem or personality by themselves that cause us challenges, but rather the emotion we experience around these which has the greatest impact. For example, having a disagreement with a work colleague because you have a personality difference is not the main issue as the reality is that you are not going to like or be liked by everyone in the world. It's when you feel exasperated, disappointed or angry and this shows in your behaviours, that the real challenges and issues arise. You may feel challenged by a dip in confidence, which on its own is okay and a natural part of life, but it is the anxiety and emotions of worry, concern and uncertainty that magnify and cause the challenge to be greater.

An example of this occurred for me at work some time ago. I was working on a team project that required a number of the team to sit around a table for extended periods of time day after day, trying to find solutions to certain problems. The team leader kept coming up behind me to look over my shoulder to check my work. As this went on I became less productive and more frustrated with the situation until I simply just got up and left the room. It wasn't until the team leader followed me out and asked me what was going on that I fully understood the situation. My team leader's action, though repetitious, was not that bad but for me it reminded me of when I was a child at school and my father would look over my shoulder while I was doing my homework. I hated this, as it represented being watched and checked on all the time, and it was only when I explained this to my team leader that he understood what was happening below the surface of my iceberg. From this we were able to clear the air, understand each other better and work more collectively in a positive manner.

We tend to see emotions as either good or bad, but the truth is that they are neither — all our emotions are there for a reason. By describing some emotions as bad you are likely training yourself to accept and judge them that way, and when we judge things we tend to add on another unpleasant emotion. Rather than judging your emotions as either good or bad, try looking at them as either pleasant or unpleasant. It's okay to feel sad, happy, angry, elated, frustrated, surprised, etc., as these and other emotions are all there to help and support us through the many facets of our life. Some emotions are unpleasant, however, when used in the right manner they can motivate us to act. For example, if you feel anxious about taking a driving test then this anxiousness hopefully will motivate you to learn all the road rules and material necessary to gain more confidence and pass the test.

## Moderating your response

It will come as no surprise that as individuals our own personal behaviour makes perfect sense to us, however, when we see other people's behaviour we might simply not understand it or we judge it. A key tool to help us not judge people's behaviour is to moderate our first response to the behaviour you may see. For example, if someone at work snaps at you for no apparent reason, the chances are there is something going on under the surface in their iceberg that you simply don't know about. Instead of allowing your emotions to rise to the surface and possibly take you down a path of firing back a response that may inflame the situation, take a few deep breathes and while doing so say to yourself, 'Something must be going on in their iceberg.' By taking some time to think about and moderating our responses we can avoid emotions that could lead us to unhelpful behaviours.

---

By aiming to understand what goes on in other people's icebergs we are able to gain a greater respect and understanding of their values and motivations, while also growing our own emotional awareness, empathy, communications and relationships. Add to this the tool of moderating our response to behaviours that don't make sense to us and we can become less judgemental and more in control of our behaviours that may be unhelpful.

Iceberg key points:

+ There are no good or bad emotions — it's only the behaviour that stems from them that can be classified as good/bad.

+ Aim to view emotions as helpful or unhelpful rather than good or bad.

+ Attitude is formed by a complex web of beliefs, values and traits that lie beneath the surface of our iceberg.

+ Often it's not the values or beliefs by themselves that cause us challenges, it is the emotion that we experience around them.

+ Do you judge the behaviour of others based on the 10 per cent you see and not the 90 per cent you don't?

+ Moderate your first response to the behaviour you see to control emotions that may lead to unhelpful behaviour on your part.

## The Happiness Pie

The search for what truly makes us happy has been an enduring challenge based on a set of powerful myths. The first myth is that you can find happiness if you search long and hard enough, and if you are lucky. The second myth is that happiness is dependent upon your circumstances. The third myth is that you either have happiness or you don't.

The Happiness Pie theory is based on research undertaken by Sonja Lyubomirsky. Her work has put these myths to rest and replaced them with a very clear picture of what determines happiness and how every one of us can have as much of it as we would like. The reason happiness is not something we can find is because it doesn't exist 'out there'. It exists within us and by changing and managing our state of mind and the way we perceive the world around us we can generate and experience the levels of happiness that we desire.

According to Lyubomirsky, the difference between how happy we are compared to others is clearly determined by three factors. The first is the influence of our genetic make-up, our DNA, which accounts for 50 per cent of our happiness. This, as we saw in the previous chapter, is our happiness set point and can't be changed.

The second factor is our circumstances. This includes what's happened to us in our past, how much money we earn, how good looking we are, what car we drive, whether we are married or divorced, what suburb or house we live in, the state of our health, whether we had a happy childhood or whether we were bullied at school, etc. The circumstances factor accounts for only 10 per cent of the difference between your own level of happiness and that of others.[2]

So between our genetic make-up and our circumstances we have accounted for 60 per cent of our Happiness Pie, which still leaves us with 40 per cent to account for.

This last piece of the pie represents the mental and behavioural habits and choices we make on a daily basis, which is collectively known as our intentional activity. Have you ever known someone who has had a difficult upbringing or negative parents yet is positive and happy in their outlook? Or on the other side, do you know someone who constantly feels they are a victim or is negative in their outlook yet they had a great childhood with lots of opportunities, coupled with energetic parents?

The notion that we are born a certain way with a pre-disposed make-up that will determine our level of happiness is simply not the case, as 40 per cent of our happiness is within our control. By focusing on that 40 per cent we can create pathways that will build resilience, and create new mental and behavioural habits to support us when times get tough so that we can bounce back with renewed meaning, purpose and happiness.

If our genetic factor (DNA) represents 50 per cent of our overall

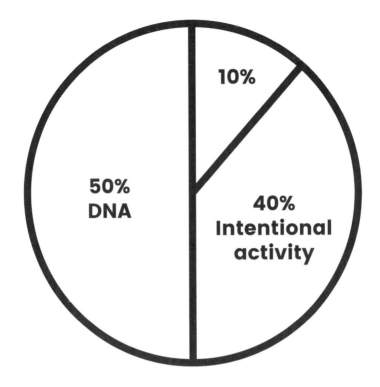

10%

50%
DNA

40%
Intentional
activity

happiness or happiness set point, and if 10 per cent represents the ups and downs of life, then focusing on the 40 per cent that represents our intentional activity can mean the difference between living above or below our happiness set point as outlined in the Chapter 2. Some interesting research studying identical twins backs this up. We sometimes take for granted that we are all unique people who are different or distinctive from each other. Identical twins challenge this concept.

Consider the story of identical twins who were brought up in a hostile and challenging environment. Their father was in gaol and their mother was an alcoholic. As a family they moved house frequently and as children the twins spent much time fending for themselves, getting their own meals and deciding on whether they would go to school or not. The only normal thing about their life was that there was no normality. As they became young men, each went off on their own path, with different outcomes. One went on to live a life similar to his mother's, moving from house to house, not being able to hold down a job for an extended period of time, having several failed relationships and ending up with an alcohol dependency. The other twin got a job making hamburgers, put himself through night school to get a qualification, got a better job, married, had two children and had a stable lifestyle. When asked why they thought their lives had turned out the way they did, both replied, 'What choice did I have? Have you seen the way I was raised?' In essence, one twin's attitude was that the way he was raised determined the rest of his life. The other twin, meanwhile, held the view that although his upbringing was not good he was determined not to allow it to dictate how the rest of his life would be, and he actively engaged in activities that increased his levels of satisfaction and happiness.[3]

## Engaging in activities to increase happiness

By engaging in activities and actions that lie within this 40 per cent of the Happiness Pie, we can increase the frequency, intensity and duration of our happiness spikes and decrease the frequency, intensity and duration of our happiness troughs, thus helping ourselves live a life well above our determined genetic set point regardless of our DNA or circumstances.

It is with this 40 per cent intentional activity that the secret to happiness lies. How you behave, what you think and the goals you set for yourself every day of your life impact on your happiness. There is no happiness without action and it's the little things you do every day that will make a difference. It's not about thinking one big thing will fill your 40 per cent, or saying to yourself, 'I'll be happy when …' as in most cases your life will pass you by while you're waiting for the big 'when' to happen. It's more about being present in the moment and focusing on the constant choices we make in how we live and what is happening right now. Creating small steps of happiness — such as stopping to take in the aroma of your morning coffee before you have your first sip, feeling the sunshine on your face, holding a piece of chocolate in your mouth and allowing it to melt over your taste buds, or appreciating the rhythm in the music you're listening to — allows us to build new and supportive mental habits and behaviours that savour positive moments and control our behaviours and actions.

By focusing more on things you can control, including thoughts, beliefs and expectations, and less on the things you can't control you will not only create the right attitude but you will have a greater chance of maximizing your 40 per cent and thus increasing your levels of happiness.

## Fixed mindset and growth mindset

Psychologist and researcher Carol Dweck, who works in the fields of motivation and positive psychology, believes the beliefs (both conscious and subconscious) and attitudes that make up our mindset have a significant impact upon the choices we make and the goals we pursue, and how changing even the simplest of these can have a profound impact on nearly every aspect of our life.

Dweck's research has shown that we hold a basic belief or mindset about ourselves that has to do with how we view and inhabit what we consider to be our personality. This mindset develops from a young age, and has an important impact on how we behave and how we handle success and failure in our lives and, ultimately, our

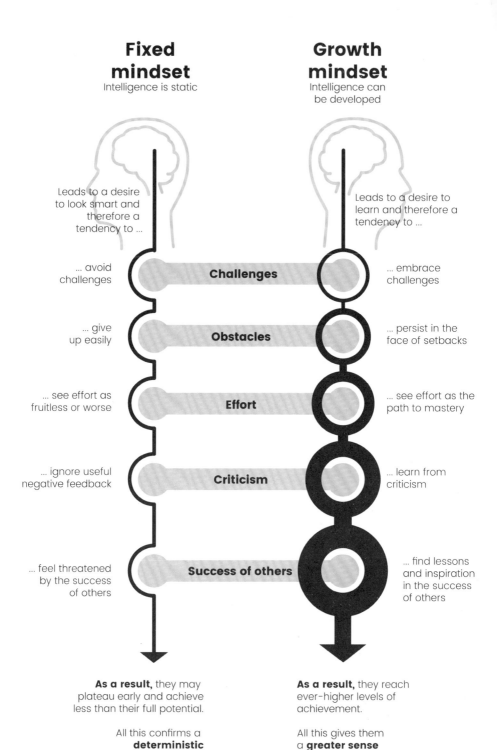

# Fixed mindset
Intelligence is static

# Growth mindset
Intelligence can be developed

Leads to a desire to look smart and therefore a tendency to ...

Leads to a desire to learn and therefore a tendency to ...

**Challenges**
... avoid challenges
... embrace challenges

**Obstacles**
... give up easily
... persist in the face of setbacks

**Effort**
... see effort as fruitless or worse
... see effort as the path to mastery

**Criticism**
... ignore useful negative feedback
... learn from criticism

**Success of others**
... feel threatened by the success of others
... find lessons and inspiration in the success of others

**As a result,** they may plateau early and achieve less than their full potential.

**As a result,** they reach ever-higher levels of achievement.

All this confirms a **deterministic view of the world.**

All this gives them a **greater sense of free will.**

capacity for happiness. Dwek differentiates between what is known as a fixed mindset and a growth mindset.

## Fixed mindset

Certain attributes are commonly perceived to be 'fixed', such as how smart you are or how talented you might be. People with a fixed mindset believe they have a certain amount of ability, talent, intelligence etc. and that this is fixed — what they have is what they have. This mindset leads people to avoid challenging their beliefs, and discourages them from trying, which therefore limits their opportunities and achievements. This can also lead to having lower expectations of others and therefore not taking opportunities to develop others as well. There is a belief that this is as good as it gets, so there is no point trying any harder as it won't make any difference. People with a fixed mindset often don't move out of their comfort zone and try to hide their deficiencies as they don't like to be seen as falling short in some way. They may potentially sabotage opportunities to develop by questioning whether they will succeed or not, or by convincing themselves that they will appear dumb if they attempt something or be rejected.

## Growth mindset

A growth mindset is built upon the belief that continuous improvement is always possible. People with this mindset believe they can always improve, learn new things, grow and develop. They believe that even basic talents and abilities can be developed over time. They are not discouraged by failure and see it as a learning experience. This leads to trying new things, welcoming challenges and striving for more.

People with this mindset also generally believe that others can, with the appropriate motivation, education or opportunities, also improve and will seek out certain opportunities to help others grow.

## What's your mindset?

We all have a fixed or growth mindset about certain things at times. Have you ever found yourself talking to a child and, from a fixed mindset, saying something along the lines of:

> 'Look at that drawing; you're going to be an artist for sure.'
>
> 'Wow, 8 out of 10! You're smart and destined for great things!'
>
> 'I suppose a C in your test is the best we could hope for.'

Alternatively, have you ever found yourself saying, from a growth mindset, something along the lines of:

> 'That picture has so many beautiful colours. Tell me about them.'
>
> 'Congratulations on the effort you put in. Let's also work together some more and figure out what you don't understand.'
>
> 'Everyone learns in a different way. Let's keep trying to find the way that works for you.'

A huge part of promoting a growth mindset is to focus your discussions or feedback on the process rather than the outcome. If you look at the example above in relation to the child's drawing, by asking the child to describe the colours in the picture you are focusing on the process. The child might talk about how she mixed certain colours to make another colour, what the colours represent and how she did the shading to create certain images. All of this creates feedback and leads the discussion around growth, development and possibilities, and engages the child in the process rather than reinforcing a fixed mindset that the picture the child drew means that they are going to be an artist.

A good way to think about having a growth mindset is to consider your brain like a muscle that grows stronger with use. Every time you stretch yourself, take on a new challenge or learn something new, your brain develops and forms new connections and you get smarter over time. By becoming comfortable and accepting that everyone (not just you) has doubts, confusion and setbacks in their lives, and by looking at the process rather than the outcome, you can over time develop a way of thinking about your own skills, talents and abilities that supports a growth mindset.

A simple tool to help you look for opportunities to create a growth mindset is outlined in the diagram below.

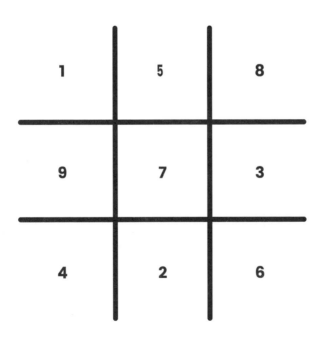

As you can see, the numbers one to nine have been placed in nine boxes. If I asked you to move the number six to where number two is and number two to where number seven is and so on, how many possibilities are there in moving nine numbers in nine boxes before you start to duplicate the same pattern and therefore run out of possibilities? The answer may surprise you, as there are more than 300,000 possibilities for moving nine numbers within nine boxes before you repeat the same pattern. On the surface this looks impossible, but following the mathematical formula of one times one through to nine, then two times one through to nine and so on, reveals that it is possible. The point is, if you look at life like the numbers in this box then you could initially say that your opportunities are limited. However, if you look a little deeper you will find that there are always more possibilities to situations than you initially imagine. Just because at first you don't see the possibility doesn't mean it's not there. By remembering this tool, you can exercise your brain and support a growth mindset to create a great attitude.

## Complete the circle

Believe it or not, many successful people have followed a simple tool made famous in the late 1800s by American billionaire John D. Rockefeller. Rockefeller believed that one of the keys to his success was that he had the discipline to place tasks in order of priority and then start with the first one and stay with it until the task was completed. He believed that it took less energy and time to finish what you had started than to stop and start again later, and that unfinished projects often caused distraction and stress. He therefore adopted the attitude of 'completing your circle'. Whatever he started he stayed with it to its conclusion, whether it be something that took a few minutes, hours, days or years.

Wherever possible, I have tried to adopt the attitude of completing my circle and have certainly noticed that a lot of the little things in life that previously distracted and annoyed me no longer do so. For example, at home if I put a load of washing in the washing machine then I'll complete the circle by hanging it out, bringing it in when it dries and distributing the clean clothes to the rooms in which they belong. If for some reason I can't complete my circle (because I put a load of washing on before I've gone to work) then I'll ensure that someone can support me, either in part or in full, to hang it out, and I'll then bring it in when I'm home and distribute the clothes to the room they need to go to. Whatever the task is, completing my circle gives me a great sense of satisfaction that I have contributed and achieved something, as well as a strong sense that my energy is being well spent on completed rather than unfinished tasks.

--- 

This chapter has looked at what attitude is — a feeling or opinion about something or someone, or a way of behaving that is caused by this — and how much of our happiness is determined by the attitude and choices we make. Our attitude can help us explore ways to become flexible, be positive, look for possibilities and be motivated by changing our mindset. Our attitude is informed by a complex web of beliefs, feelings, values and traits that lie deep within us. We form attitudes about everything we encounter, often without thinking, and sometimes we act on predetermined notions that limit us and are no longer relevant. Our attitude influences our physical and mental health. The best news is that we can learn to change our attitude no matter how old we are, often with amazing results. Attitude is a habit and since we become our habits it's important that you choose them wisely. We always have a choice in what attitude we practise, and by broadening our thinking we can build our personal attitude resources to help us be more motivated, productive and happier.

With this in mind, you may now like to take five minutes and complete the following Attitude Inventory by answering a number of multiple choice questions to see how you score. The key points listed at the end of this chapter can support you in building a stronger attitude thinking style.

### Attitude Inventory

The purpose of this short questionnaire is to provide you with an opportunity to gain an insight into how your attitude might be playing out for you. While the questionnaire is built with best-practice frameworks, it is not designed to be a valid scientific reflection.

Take care in the way you review your results; they are best used as a conversation piece to explore positive actions that can be taken to further orient yourself towards a more positive and flourishing approach to your personal and/or professional life.

Below are seven statements. To what extent do you agree with each of these statements? Please use the following scale to indicate how much you agree with each statement:

+ Strongly agree        = 1 point
+ Somewhat agree        = 2 points
+ Not really sure       = 3 points
+ Somewhat disagree     = 4 points
+ Strongly disagree     = 5 points

| Statement | Score |
|---|---|
| 1. People who are not good at something should just avoid doing it often. | |
| 2. There is no point trying to become good at something you are just not born to do. | |
| 3. Those who get straight As easily don't need to waste time studying hard. | |
| 4. Some people are just lucky to be born a natural; others are not so lucky. | |
| 5. You can do things differently but the important parts of who you are can't really be changed. | |
| 6. You can always learn new things but you can't change how smart you are. | |
| 7. It's easier to choose not to compete than it is to try at something you know you are no good at. | |
| Total | |

Insights to consider

Now tally up your score from the questionnaire.

**Higher score (25–35)**

You may tend to approach challenges with gusto and openness, not always expecting to be great but open to learning and growing. You may also tend to give others more chances at trying things, and be motivated to give them the same growth opportunity. You are more likely to seek out and embrace feedback from experts who do well at things you are trying.

**Mid-range score (16–24)**

You may find that there are particular environments or people with whom you have a much more positive attitude. There may be others where you are quick to jump to conclusions. It is worth reflecting upon when your mindset differs so you can adjust where required.

**Lower score (5–15)**

You may tend to jump to conclusions about your potential or that of others and not take up opportunities to participate in some activities. You may also avoid situations where you have a fear of failing. You may overlook some people for opportunities because you believe they can't succeed. You may also tend not to be open to feedback from others who are performing better than you.

# To sum up

The key points and tools from this chapter for our ORANGES toolkit are:

+ Attitude is something we bring to every situation.
+ Your thinking style is the key to boosting resilience.
+ We tend to see emotions as either good or bad, but the truth is that they are neither as all our emotions are there for a reason.
+ The notion that we are born a certain way, with a pre-disposed make-up that will determine our level of happiness, is simply not the case as 40 per cent of our happiness is within our control.
+ By focusing on the 40 per cent we can create pathways that will build resilience, and create new mental and behavioural habits to support us when times get tough so that we can bounce back with renewed meaning, purpose and happiness.
+ Our mindset is our attitude towards things and influences our behaviour.
+ Remember the possibilities of nine numbers in nine boxes to help create a growth mindset.
+ Complete your circle.
+ Make choices that will reinforce a positive attitude in yourself and others.
+ Praise people for the effort they put in and the challenges they overcome more than their traits.

# 4

## Now

**Now** (*noun*) At the present time or moment.

> Be happy in the moment, that's enough. Each moment is
> all we need, not more.
>
> **Mother Teresa**

Living in the now means focusing on and enjoying the present moment. It's about training ourselves to be more mindful so we can put things in perspective and gain more emotional control.

Now, is literally being in the now, being fully present and focused so that you can be more aware of your surroundings, behaviours and conversations.

When we approach the world with mindful awareness we pay close attention to what is happening moment by moment. This helps us more accurately assess and respond to situations and people. By noticing and separating ourselves from old beliefs and anxieties, we become more accepting of ourselves and other people. Mindfulness is therefore the opposite of mindlessness, which we have all experienced at some stage. For example, have you ever driven somewhere and arrived at your destination and not remembered passing through a certain set of traffic lights or really anything about the journey itself? That's mindlessness — it's when we operate on autopilot. Ellen Langer's research into mindlessness shows, among other things, that it's the mindless processing of information and our interpretation of its use to us, as well as a belief that we have limited resources and skills, that limits our ability to be mindful or support sound decision-making.[1]

The practice of mindfulness involves resting our awareness in one place for an extended period of time without being distracted. It has three main qualities: relaxation (settling the body in its natural state); stillness (avoiding movement to quieten the mind); and vigilance (careful, focused attention on the mind itself, moment by moment).

While this skill takes time to learn and discipline to practise to make a good habit, it doesn't take long to make real progress and the benefits are immediate. Followers of Buddhism and other spiritual traditions have been practising mindfulness for over 2500 years and science now recognizes the enormous positive effect it can have on our mental and physical health, relationships, happiness, decision-making and learning.

A preliminary study at the University of California takes this even further and suggests a link between the mind wandering and cellular ageing. The study focused on DNA telomere length, a biomarker of overall bodily ageing. Shorter telomeres indicate ageing while longer telomeres indicate greater longevity. Within the study, assessments were carried out on whether participants had the tendency to remain in the present moment or allow their minds to wonder and lose focus. Present-moment awareness (or being in the now) was defined as being focused on the task at hand, while mind wandering was described as having your thoughts elsewhere or not being in the now. The results showed that participants who recorded having greater focus and being present in the moment had longer telomeres and therefore slower ageing and increased longevity.[2] The study recognized that practising mindfulness helped participants learn about their current thoughts and emotional state while increasing awareness. It allowed participants to concentrate on their inner wellbeing rather than focusing on external influences, and therefore the participant was able to consider personal acceptance of the moment without fear of judgement or being weighed down with expectations.

Other studies have shown the link between our overall happiness and wellbeing are closely aligned to our ability to be present in the moment no matter what you are doing. Harvard researcher Matt Killingsworth's work took a large sample group of 15,000 people throughout 80 countries with varying levels of age, education, occupation and economic status. The study revealed that what made people happy had far less to do with what activity they were doing at any given moment but more to do with whether their attention was fully present in the moment of that activity.[3] The people who were mindful and present within the activity they were doing were significantly happier than those who let their minds wander away from the activity they were in. It didn't matter what the activity was;

even if it was deemed annoying or awful, people were still happier when they fully engaged their attention in the moment.

According to Killingsworth's research, within a day the average person's mind wanders approximately 47 per cent of the time and it's within this time that we can become vulnerable to negative emotions, self-doubt, anxiety and depression.[4] The research backs up what spiritual traditions have long been telling us: that the key to happiness and wellbeing depends not on the external circumstances in our lives but more so on the state of our minds, on being aware and responsive to one's surroundings. Put simply, are we aware of what is going on in our body, in our mind and our emotional state and how this impacts us?

There are some amazing benefits to being focused and present in the moment, and the tools outlined in this chapter can assist you in broadening your thinking and building your personal mindfulness resources. Increased mindfulness and focus can:

+ give you richer experiences
+ help you notice things more
+ increase the accuracy of your perceptions
+ support your curiosity to finding out more
+ sharpen your memory and recall
+ increase your emotional control
+ strengthen your immune system
+ help improve your relationships.

## The myth of multitasking

Contrary to popular belief we are not hardwired to effectively do multiple jobs all at once. Humans are certainly not capable of handling multiple actions or tasks in quick succession, or mixing actions or tasks that have become habit-forming with those that are not so automatic. That's why driving your car and texting is not a good idea as you simply can't effectively attend to two things at once without putting yourself in possible danger.

The first step towards building a stronger mindfulness practice is to acknowledge that, try as you might, you can really only do one thing at a time with any effectiveness. If this is the case then aim to put your energies in to that one thing. Of the 47 per cent of the time when our minds wander, most of it is used either thinking about the past or the future. We pass through the moment we're in and end up either going backwards or trying to go forwards, and this potentially leaves us with a feeling that life has passed us by. Thinking about the past can be problematic, as it can't be changed. We can certainly change our relationship and emotion to the past but we can't undo what has been done. And thinking about the future is tricky, as we often have no control over the other influences that may or may not have an impact on how things will pan out.

## Meditation

To help us stay present and not get distracted we need to build on our mindfulness practices so that we can learn to rest our awareness in one place for extended periods of time. And to do this we need to achieve the three main qualities of mindfulness that were mentioned earlier:

+ Relaxation: settling the body in its natural state. The ability to relax the body, muscles and physical sensations from head to toe.
+ Stillness: avoiding movement to quieten the mind. Bringing all physical activities of the body to rest and all mental activities of the mind to rest.
+ Vigilance: careful, focused attention on the mind itself, moment by moment. Heightened awareness of moment-by-moment experiences.

One tool that covers these three qualities is meditation, and it can come in many different forms. Even Buddha, whose own efforts led him to enlightenment, knew this and the *Abhidhamma*, an ancient Buddhist text, indicates that it's not a one-size-fits-all approach; rather, people should be taught and learn according to their individual needs.

You don't need to sit cross-legged in the lotus position on top of a mountain as sometimes portrayed, nor do you need to make chanting sounds like a Tibetan monk. Meditation can be done individually or in a group, within your own home, at work or even standing in line at the supermarket. As with any kind of exercise you should start off easy and gradually build on the amount of time you meditate. Meditation should be viewed as a lifelong tool that you constantly develop, rather than something you do spasmodically or seen as a quick fix. Some people suggest fifteen to twenty minutes each day while others advocate a few times a week. Whether it's five to ten minutes, more than half an hour, a couple of times a week or every day the overall advice is simply to make sure you do what works for you and make it into a habit.

At work, we have introduced mindfulness sessions on a regular basis and created an atmosphere where it's okay for people to stop work and take some time out from their busy schedules. Being a multi-sited national organization means sessions are usually held over Skype or teleconference, so no matter where people are (at their work station, on their mobile phone or working from home) they can participate. The sessions, though voluntary to attend, are run by someone experienced and are generally well attended as the participants realize that the ten to fifteen minutes they set aside during their work day actually allows them to be more productive for the rest of the day. The staff state that through mindfulness they are generally more aware of what is going on around them, are less stressed and are more engaged with their work.

## A mindfulness activity

If you have five minutes to spare then try this short mindfulness activity. To make it easier you may want to slowly read and record the following script into your phone then find somewhere to sit comfortably or even lie down on the floor. Start by simply focusing on the room you are in and the space around you. As you are doing this take some breaths through your nose and out through your mouth to commence a rhythm of your breath. After your first four or five breaths make the next four or five breaths loud as you breathe in and out so that if someone else was in the room they would hear you. Now conduct a simple body check and acknowledge how you are feeling: is your body relaxed or are any of your muscles feeling tight? Is your mind clear or do you feel tired? Do you feel energized or are you tense? Whatever it is you acknowledge it, try to just let it go and soften your mind and your body each time you exhale.

Now gently close your eyes and follow these steps:

+ Bring your attention to your breathing and try to use this as your anchor. If your attention wanders during the exercise, simply bring it gently back to focus on your breath.

+ Notice the air as it comes in through your nostrils and goes down to the bottom of your lungs. Then notice or follow it as it goes back out again.

+ Feel the sensation of your body resting and follow the air as if you're riding the waves of your breathing.

+ Notice the air moving in and out of your nostrils. Does it feel slightly warmer as in comes out and cooler as it goes in?

+ Notice the rise and fall of your ribcage.

+ Notice the gentle rise and fall of your stomach.

+ As you bring your mind into the body fix your attention on one of these areas of breathing, whichever one you prefer. Keep the attention on this spot and notice the movement of your breath, ribcage or stomach.

+ Whatever feelings, urges, sensations or thoughts arise, whether pleasant or unpleasant, gently acknowledge them as if nodding your head to someone as you pass them by in the street. Acknowledge their presence but do not engage with them or judge them, and let them go by putting your attention back onto your breath.

+ From time to time your attention will become distracted by thoughts or feelings. Each time this happens, notice what distracted you then bring your attention back to your breath. No matter how often your attention wanders off, whether a few times or many, simply notice what it is that distracted you and bring your attention back to your breath.

+ There is no need to be frustrated, impatient or disappointed when you mind is carried off by your thoughts. It's the same for everyone. Our minds naturally distract us from what we are doing, so each time you realize your attention has wandered, gently acknowledge it, notice what distracted you and return your attention back to your breath.

+ Keep the attention on this spot and try to keep this as your anchor.

+ If frustration, boredom, impatience or other feelings arise simply acknowledge them and return your focus on your breath, keeping your attention on your chosen area of the body.

+ When you are ready, bring your attention back to the room and open your eyes. You may even want to have a big stretch.

Now that you are back in the room, do another body check and see how you feel and if there is a difference. If you were feeling tension before doing the breath exercise, has some of that tense feeling gone?

Do you feel a bit more relaxed? Has your heart rate slowed down and does your mind feel a bit clearer?

## Flow

Flow (also known as being 'in the zone') occurs when you are completely involved in an activity, when your whole being is interested, you are fully immersed in a feeling of invigorated focus and you are using your skills to the utmost. Every action, movement and thought follows from the one before. It can happen solving a puzzle, playing sport, negotiating a business deal or when deep in conversation with someone. You are completely absorbed in doing something and time seems to fly by.

The concept of flow is the culmination of over twenty years of study by Mihaly Csikszentmihalyi, a renowned Professor of Psychology, into the state of optimal experiences, what makes us happy and when it is we're most happy. According to Csikszentmihalyi, flow is completely focused motivation that challenges our self in harnessing our emotions and skills in the pursuit of performing and learning. It broadens our thinking and allows our positive emotions to be challenged and energized to the task at hand, often resulting in a feeling of great pleasure, happiness and even rapture.

People can experience flow in many ways and what you may experience might be different to others. Some people might experience it at work solving a difficult problem, some may get it when painting or writing music, while others may get it playing a sport or when engaged in a physical challenge.[5]

A colleague of mine loves body surfing and one day she told me about her weekend and how her family had gone to the beach. The waves that day were big and powerful, with set after set rolling in to the shore. She and her brother agreed to body surf for half an hour while other family members looked after the children. With a nod they both headed to the water's edge to start the journey of swimming out beyond the breaking waves and into deep water. The thrill of catching the waves excited her and once she was out in the water she was able to ascertain that though the waves were strong in force and size and they would certainly challenge her, her skills were good enough to be tested. She spoke with passion on how, with great concentration, she caught the first wave perfectly, rolling down the face of it like sliding on ice. While everything was travelling fast she spoke of how riding the wave seemed to go for an eternity, when in reality it may have been only five to ten seconds. She felt in control and able to adjust and adapt to the different challenges each wave threw at her. She was getting constant feedback through the thrill of riding the wave to the end, and when she misjudged a wave and got dumped she was able to learn from it and adjust her actions accordingly for the next wave. She told me that she hadn't noticed her brother had gone and was back on the beach, and it was only when she headed in that she realized how tired and hungry she was becoming. To her even greater surprise, when she got back to her family she learned that her original time of a half-hour swim had actually turned into a couple of hours. She had become so immersed in her activity and so focused in the moment that she completely lost track of all time. She had experienced flow.

According to Csikszentmihalyi there are ten chief characteristics that accompany the experience of being in flow or in the zone.

+ The activity you are doing has clear goals that challenge you but are still attainable.
+ The activity requires dedicated concentration and focus.
+ It is intrinsically rewarding.

+ There is a loss of self-consciousness.
+ You lose track of time or have a distorted sense of time.
+ You receive immediate feedback.
+ You can work out the balance required between the challenge you are facing and the skills required by you.
+ You feel comfortable that you are able to control the situation.
+ You experience a lack of awareness of physical needs.
+ There is a complete focus on the activity and nothing else.[6]

While many of these characteristics will be present when you are experiencing a moment of flow, it's not necessary for all ten to be present at once for flow to occur. Flow can happen as part of our everyday life whether at home, at work, on the sports field or at school and we can actually create opportunities for flow by simply challenging and stretching ourselves slightly beyond our current skill level. For example, at school you might challenge yourself to study a subject ranked the next grade up from the level you are at now. At work, you may arrange your day so that you can solely focus on one activity, whether it be writing a report or creating a presentation; or on the sporting field you might set yourself a challenge that is doable but hasn't been reached yet, like playing a round of golf with one less stroke than your previous best.

By being challenged with an activity that is a stretch but is still attainable, we can learn to focus our minds and harness our emotions and skills to attain flow. This will not only create great joy and happiness for us but enable further learning, skill development and improved performance.

# Curiosity

Another tool to help support you in being more mindful and focused and to enjoy the present moment is curiosity. In order to be present you need to be curious, as curiosity supports moment-by-moment experiences and engages us. It creates an openness to unfamiliar experiences, allowing us to explore more opportunities to discover and experience surprise, joy and happiness. Curiosity has been recognized as a main motivator that influences human behaviour (either positively or negatively) at every stage of our life, and with practice it can be nurtured and harnessed to occur in our everyday life to great effect. It's a driving force behind our physical, mental and emotional development, as well as being the catalyst behind many problem-solving and scientific discoveries and the creation of great music and literature. Being curious gives you the strength to be open and accepting of whatever is happening in the present. It allows you to approach new experiences and events with a mindful awareness, whether that is the positive and beautiful or the challenging and upsetting.

Research shows that there are a number of ways curiosity enhances our wellbeing. Professor of Psychology Todd Kashdan states that if we are able to dial up our curiosity, it can have a positive influence on decreasing any anxiety we may be feeling. Kashdan believes we should acknowledge the existence of anxiety in our lives and, when faced with this, turn up the dial on the other side of the equation, which is being curious. 'Our curiosity and threat detection systems evolved together, and they are functions to ensure optimal decisions are made in an unpredictable world,' he writes. 'We are all motivated by the pull toward safety and seek to avoid danger, but we all possess a fundamental motivation to expand and grow as human beings.'[7]

Kashdan's work outlines how curiosity and interest can transform stress, fear and pain and build elements that are more conducive to a meaningful life.

One tool Kashdan advocates is spending a few minutes a day being curious beyond your normal daily routine — choose an activity to do that you haven't done before, take a different route to work and look at your surroundings, start up a conversation with someone you don't know or try brushing your teeth with your other hand and see how you go.

A few years back I decided I would make a point each year to undertake an activity that would take some time to master while also allowing me to be curious. Something I didn't have to do every day but still regularly enough for me to learn and master over time. One year I taught myself to juggle and to see how many balls I could juggle at once by the end of the year, and how many different styles of juggling I could learn. Another year I took up a sport I hadn't played and became curious as to its rules and rituals, and recently I've taken up beekeeping and now have a hive in my backyard, about which I've become completely curious and fascinated with how bees work together and make honey. Over the years, each one of these activities has added an enormous amount of positivity and enjoyment to my life (that's not to say that there haven't been periods of frustration and feelings that I haven't had a clue what I was doing) and have substantially increased my levels of being present in the moment or, in other words, being mindful.

Some of the other ways curiosity enhances our lives are discussed in more detail on the next page.

## Health

In a study published in *Psychology and Aging*, researchers over a five-year period followed 1000 adults aged 60 to 86 and found (even taking into consideration factors such as age, education, social circumstances and health) that those who were attributed as being more curious at the commencement of the study were more likely to be alive at its completion, five years later.[8]

## Intelligence

A study published in the *Journal of Personality and Social Psychology* in 2002, stated that researchers evaluated 1795 three-year-olds to see how curious they were. From this, researchers accurately predicted that the three-year-olds who rated higher in the curiosity evaluations would have further advanced IQs as older children than the three-year-olds who were evaluated with lower levels of curiosity.[9] This finding supports others that have found curiosity leads to and supports a growth mindset. It has also been discovered that there is a basic circuit in the brain that energizes people to go out and get things that are intrinsically rewarding. Psychologists Charan Ranganath and Dr Matthias Gruber, of the University of California, have found that this circuit becomes active when we get things that appeal directly to us such as food, money or emotional connection. It also activates when we become curious and releases a natural chemical called dopamine, which improves the contact between cells connected with learning and gives us a natural high.[10] Research has also shown that those who are more curious are more likely to remember things.[11]

## Social engagement

Many studies demonstrate the link between happiness and the actual number of friends or companions people report, as well as the social support and companionship they experience and perceive. This is not surprising when you consider that relationships are considered by social scientists as the most important factor in our survival as a species, and curiosity plays an important role in maintaining relationships.[12] For example, a longitudinal study examined photos in yearbooks from high schools and evaluated the happiness of female students based on the quality of their smiles. The women were followed up twenty years after their high school photos. Those who had been evaluated as having a genuine high-quality smile in their yearbook photo were found to be far more satisfied with their lives, had low divorce rates, were more curious and had a large network of friends.[13]

## Happiness

The Gallup organization conducted a worldwide survey modelled to equal 96 per cent of the world's population through the involvement of 130,000 people from 130 countries. In aiming to ascertain how much pleasure and enjoyment was experienced by the individual on any given day, the survey found out that 'being able to count on someone for help' and 'learning something new' where the two top influences linked to an individual's level of enjoyment.[14] Both of these are supported by curiosity and confirm that developing good relationships and broadening your thinking are fundamental factors in having a happy life.

## Altruism

Studies show happy people are generally more curious, have relatively greater interest in helping people and tend to act in a prosocial or cooperative manner (i.e. they enjoy sharing or helping others). These people believed in and set out to undertake regular selfless acts of support at work by helping others, despite their own heavy workloads.[15]

# Savouring

This is a simple tool you can use anywhere and at any time that brings together mindfulness and curiosity in one activity. It can be practised on anything but for the purposes of this exercise I would like you to get either a Lindt chocolate ball (or any chocolate that's wrapped) or if you don't like chocolate then maybe a piece of fruit like an orange.

The purpose of this exercise is to focus on using all of your senses. First, place the chocolate or fruit in front of you on a table. Focus 100 per cent on the item in front of you. During this exercise all sorts of thoughts and feelings will distract you; simply acknowledge them and quietly let them go just as we did during the meditation exercise, and bring your focus back to the chocolate. Now pick up the chocolate in one hand and slowly look at it from all angles. Turn it around and look at it from all sides. Notice the texture of the wrapper, how many colours and shades it has, whether it has a pattern, design or logo on it. Notice the weight of it: does it feel heavy or light, solid or hollow?

+ Now hold the chocolate up to your ear and give it a shake. Does it rattle or make a sound? Can you make the wrapper rustle by rubbing your fingers across it? Gently give it a squeeze, and note if it feels hard or slightly soft.

+ Now slowly unwrap the chocolate, taking your time to see how the wrapping has been folded together. Is it one piece of wrapping or are there more? How big is the wrapping and does it have a certain shape? Take the chocolate and hold it up to the light, noticing if you can you see through it or if is it solid, if the light shines off it, if it is rough on the outside or smooth. Take it to your nose and smell it, and note what it smells like. Now rest the chocolate against your lips: is it starting to melt against your skin? Slowly put it in your mouth and hold it there for five seconds without chewing or biting. Is it starting to melt or is it remaining solid? Try to hold it in your mouth for as long as possible without biting into it. Notice what's happening inside your mouth. Do you have any salivation, an anticipation and urge to bite into it?

+ Now see if you can bite into half of it and allow the other half to remain in your mouth. Close your eyes to enhance the experience and notice any urges you have.

+ Roll the remaining chocolate around inside your mouth and notice the taste and texture. Can you feel the chocolate covering your teeth? Notice what your jaw is doing right now.

+ Now bite into the remainder of the chocolate and listen to see if it makes any sound inside your mouth. Swallow the remainder of the chocolate and see if you can feel it sliding down your throat, noticing the sensations.

Once you have finished your chocolate (or fruit), spend some time reflecting on what you experienced. Did the chocolate taste better? Did you feel more satisfied after eating one piece? Did you feel any different or more prolonged sensations? Did you notice something about the chocolate or wrapper that you had never really seen before? From this activity we can see how easy it can be to utilize our senses to increase our day to day experiences. Whether it be walking the dog and listening to the sounds around you, washing the dishes and feeling your hands soften in the water or doing some gardening and feeling the warmth of the sun we all have the opportunity to increase our awareness. By savouring these positive experiences we get to be present and enjoy life's moments more often, and for longer.

--- 

This chapter has looked at the present time or moment, the 'now', and how focusing on the present moment, being mindful, is a special tool that can help us pay attention to enhance and cope with everyday life. Many people spend much time thinking over things that have happened in the past or worrying about things that may happen in the future, to the point that they forget to enjoy and appreciate the moment they are actually in. Living in the present moment will not eliminate life's challenges and the pressures we face; however, it can assist us to respond to these from a mental, physical or emotional perspective in a calmer and more positive manner. It allows us to move away from everyday life and creates a space that can help us to flourish. The science overwhelmingly supports the benefits of being present in the moment, maintaining moments of flow, enhancing your curiosity, savouring and stretching the moment you're in. It's about living your life as if it really matters, moment by moment, and you can increase your awareness and mindfulness every day through activities like meditation, being observant, yoga, taking time to savour a moment or simply paying more attention to your surroundings when walking or driving. The tools you use and how long you them for is up to you; the main thing is to start and keep practising so that you broaden your thinking and build the personal resources that will wake you up to the rewards, adventures and meaning in life's moments.

With this in mind, you may now like to take five minutes and complete the following Now Inventory by answering a number of multiple choice questions to see how you score and how the key points listed at the end of this chapter can support you in building a stronger mindful thinking style.

## Now Inventory

The purpose of this short questionnaire is to provide you with an opportunity to gain an insight into how mindfulness may be playing out for you. While the questionnaire is built with best-practice frameworks, it is not designed to be a valid scientific reflection.

Take care in the way you review your results; they are best used as a conversation piece to explore positive actions that can be taken to further orient yourself towards a more positive and flourishing approach to your personal and/or professional life.

Below are seven statements. To what degree are these statements like you? Please use the following scale to indicate how much like you each statement is.

+ Definitely not like me    = 1 point
+ Not much like me    = 2 points
+ Not really sure    = 3 points
+ Somewhat like me    = 4 points
+ Definitely like me    = 5 points

| Statement | Score |
|---|---|
| 1. Even when I am very busy I can always be fully present when I am with someone. | |
| 2. I never have trouble with my mind wandering to other things during meetings or conversations. | |
| 3. I love it when I get spare time to just sit and contemplate things with no pressure to do anything else. | |
| 4. Very rarely am I racing around trying to find my keys, my wallet or where I put the shopping list. | |
| 5. I never get impatient with people who take a long time to explain something or tell a story. | |
| 6. I rarely forget what I am supposed to be doing or what I have promised I will do. | |
| 7. I often notice things before others do. | |
| Total | |

Insights to consider

Now tally up your score from the questionnaire.

### Higher score (25–35)

You are likely to be described as mostly calm when there is a lot going on. You may also find it easy to stay balanced when feeling overwhelmed. You may be able to process many tasks and challenges while others are running around all over the place.

### Mid-range score (16–24)

You may find that your levels of mindfulness fluctuate: sometimes you find it easy to be fully present while at other times you may find it more difficult. Exploring what factors might contribute to higher or lower levels of presence would be valuable.

### Lower score (5–15)

You could tend to spend a lot of time repeating thoughts or tasks because you lose track of where you are up to. You may find that you miss things in some conversations because your mind has wandered off. You may also suffer from 'busyness' but not 'productivity'.

# To sum up

The key points and tools from this chapter for our ORANGES toolkit are:

+ We can apply mindfulness techniques to help us every day.
+ Being in the moment and being present is important in fostering mindfulness.
+ Meditation can come in many different forms and takes practice.
+ Relaxation: settling the body in its natural state. It is the ability to relax the body, muscles and physical sensations from head to toe.
+ Stillness: avoiding movement to quieten the mind. During stillness all physical and mental activities are brought to rest.
+ Vigilance: careful, focused attention on the mind, moment by moment. It involves heightened awareness of moment-by-moment experiences.
+ The average person's mind wanders approximately 47 per cent of the time and it's within this time that we can become vulnerable to negative emotions, self-doubt, anxiety and depression.
+ Flow occurs when you are completely involved within an activity, your whole being is interested, you are fully immersed in a feeling of invigorated focus and you are using your skills to the utmost.
+ Dial up your curiosity to dial down anxieties. Turn tension into interest by asking questions and practising curiosity to seek the information you need.
+ Savouring is a simple tool you can use anywhere and at any time. It brings together mindfulness and curiosity in one activity and extends the moment you are experiencing.

# 5

## Gratitude

**Gratitude** (*noun*) The quality of being thankful, the readiness to show appreciation for and to return kindness.

> Piglet noticed that even though he had a very small heart, it could hold a rather large amount of gratitude.
>
> ***Winnie-the-Pooh**, A.A. Milne*

Picture if you will a box you can hold in the palm of your hand. When wrapped up like a gift it may look something like this:

Imagine holding this gift in your hand. What's inside may surprise you — it could be something as small as a grain of sand or as large as a mobile phone. Now I want you to imagine you can feel the weight of the gift — does it feel heavy or does it feel light?

Can you feel the texture of the paper on the outside — is it rough or smooth? Have a close look at the paper: does it have a pattern on it or is it plain? Does the ribbon feel smooth and silky between your fingers? Hold the gift near your ear. Give it a small shake; does the gift inside move and rattle or is it solid?

This is a gift that will surprise and intrigue you, as once opened it has the power to expand over and over or shrink away to nothing. Some believe its power is mysterious, however the only mystery will be in how you handle owning this gift.

You may choose to share this gift or keep it to yourself — it will make no difference to the gift itself. But be warned: how it is used can determine whether life will be better or worse. Maybe by now you are wondering what gift awaits you inside the box, but before you open it you need to know that it may arouse emotions in you like you have never felt before. It can bring tears to those who don't cry and happiness to those who feel sad. It can challenge you, excite you, motivate you and connect you like never before; it can scare you, terrify you, puzzle you and make you nervous. Almost everybody has this gift. Some use it every day, others regularly and some people seldom or never use it, opting to keep it in the box in which it came. The strange thing about this gift is that you can't buy it. You won't find it advertised in a shopping catalogue or for sale on eBay or Amazon.

You can't order it online, it doesn't come with a logo or a range of colours and you can't pay it off over a period of time.

Now picture yourself pulling back the ribbon and paper of the gift and slowly opening the box. You'll see that what's inside is simply the gift of gratitude. Whether through words, actions, money, resources, commitment or giving of your time, by committing to the gift of gratitude you can change lives. This is the opportunity I'm presenting to you.

I know you must be interested in gratitude otherwise you wouldn't be reading this chapter, so what I'm asking of you is to really commit to the expression of gratitude in whatever way works best for you. By doing this you can contribute to the gift that just keeps on giving and you can grow this gift hundreds of time over. Even though what I ask of you right now may excite, scare or challenge you, simply consider not leaving this gift within its box and believe that this opportunity might, just might, change a life.

Gratitude creates a sense of deep appreciation for what we have in life. It makes us aware of the good things that happen and connects us to a sense of life's wonder, which in turn makes us more thankful. When we appreciate something it increases in value to us, and we are more able to realize its full potential and worth. If you appreciate someone for something they have done, you both experience more positive emotions. However, gratitude doesn't require a return action. There is no distraction or diminishing return for appreciation. Thanking others makes us more tolerant of differences, creating a sense of camaraderie and belonging. As a result, gratitude connects us to something larger than ourselves, whether this is with other people, a god or higher power, or nature.

Researchers associate gratitude with psychological growth and a coping style known as positive reinterpretation.[1] When people with high levels of appreciation experience significant life changes, like surviving cancer, they are more likely to value the experience and feel glad it happened.[2] Constant appreciation of new and positive changes in our lives such as passing a test, completing a challenging task or losing weight offsets the natural propensity of us falling back to the previous levels of happiness within a year. Rather than taking happy events and successes for granted, continuing to remind ourselves why they made us feel good in the first place makes us happier for longer.[3]

This shows us why gratitude is one of the most powerful antidotes to negative emotions and depression. Research indicates that the general health and resilience of people increases when they frequently write about things that they are thankful for.[4] The more we reflect on what we are grateful for, the more we broaden our thinking and build our emotional and social resources. Acknowledging and sharing moments of gratitude is a powerful practice and tool for staying positive, energized, optimistic and resilient.

In fact, gratitude may be one of the most overlooked tools we have and can access every day. Practising gratitude certainly doesn't have to take up much time, nor does it have to cost you any money, but it can have a profound effect for both the receiver and giver and the benefits are significant.

## The benefits of gratitude

Research reveals that gratitude can have the following benefits.

### Sleep

A study in 2011 found that spending a few minutes writing down things you are grateful for that day before retiring to bed can help you sleep longer and better.[5]

## Physical health

A 2012 study published in *Personality and Individual Differences* showed that grateful people experienced fewer aches and pains and were generally physically healthier and suffered less mental fatigue than other people. The study also showed that grateful people tended to take care of their health more by exercising more often and having regular check-ups with their doctors, which contributed to further longevity.[6]

## Improved empathy and reduced aggression

A 2012 study at the University of Kentucky showed that participants who received a higher level classification on the gratitude scale showed and experienced greater understanding and rapport towards other people and lower ambition to seek retaliation. These people were also more likely to behave in a prosocial manner, even when others around them behaved less so.[7]

## Building relationships

A 2014 study published in *Emotion* found that thanking a new acquaintance makes them more likely to seek an ongoing relationship.[8] Whether you thank the person who made you your morning coffee on the way to work, thank someone for holding a door open for you, thank the person who let you merge your car into traffic or send a thank you note to someone for helping you out, acknowledging the input or support of other people can lead to new opportunities. In other words, showing gratitude can lead to broadening the circle of people you know.

## Self-esteem

A 2014 study published in the *Journal of Applied Sport Psychology* found that gratitude increased an athlete's self-esteem and confidence, which is a critical factor in optimising peak performance.[9] Other studies have shown that gratitude reduces social comparison, and that grateful people don't feel anger towards others who may have more money, bigger house or better status through their job.[10] Instead, they are able to simply appreciate other people's accomplishments.

## Improved mental health

A 2006 study published in *Behaviour Research and Therapy* found that Vietnam War veterans with higher levels of gratitude experienced lower levels of post-traumatic stress disorder.[11] Further, a 2003 study found that gratitude was a significant contributor to resilience following the September 11 terrorist attacks in the United States.[12] The study showed that even during the worst of times, being thankful and grateful fosters resilience.

## Emotional health

Robert A. Emmons PhD, a leading gratitude researcher, has undertaken many studies on the association between gratitude and people's overall wellbeing. His research confirms that gratitude reduces a multitude of toxic emotions such as hatred, envy, frustration and spite and confirms that it effectively reduces depression while supporting a happier life.[13]

# Tools to nurture gratitude

We know that expressing gratitude and appreciation can increase our levels of overall wellbeing individually and in others. Our appreciation can be extended to things other than people or acts to include areas such as the arts, beauty or experiences, or even something that grows in value like growth in the stock market to growth in a relationship.

Gratitude allows us to be thankful for what we have instead of always striving for something new in the hope that it will make us happier (i.e. 'I'll be happier when I get that promotion' or 'My life will be happier when I buy that new car'). When we appreciate something it increases in value for us and we are then able to acknowledge its full worth.

The following tools will broaden your thinking and build your personal resources so you can experience gratitude in your life on a daily basis.

## Three best things — gratitude journal

For this activity you will need a pen and a notebook you can write in. Start by taking a moment to be mindful, noticing what is going on in your body and how you are feeling. You might want to position yourself comfortably, then take a few deep breathes and aim to relax your body.

Now think of three things for which you have been grateful today. Write them down, and take some time to consider why and how each of these made you feel. It can be anything at all, such as feeling the sunshine on your face or a compliment someone gave you at work. Some constructive questions to ask yourself during this exercise are: 'What happened to me today?', 'Who or what inspired me today?', 'What made me smile today?', 'What's the best thing that happened to me today?' Once you have completed your three things take another moment to be mindful about how you are feeling and notice if there is anything that has changed for you.

Try to do this each day and get into the habit of writing down and sharing (if you choose) what you are grateful for. The most important thing is to make this activity meaningful and not just something you feel you have to do or you do on the run. It only takes a few minutes each day and it is best if you can create a regular time to do it, such as first thing in the morning before breakfast or just before you go to bed each night. If you find after a while you start to feel stale and bored about doing your journal, as you are doing it in the same way every day and it's not creating much meaning for you, then try to change things around. Be curious and write your journal in a different place, set yourself a goal of trying to identify five things in your day that made you smile then write about those; or you may want to express your gratitude in your journal through pasting in pictures or drawings then write about those.

I have been using a gratitude journal for a while now and its impact on me has been profound in many simple ways. Firstly, I tend to sleep better at night and no longer wake up early in the morning thinking about what I need to do the next day, as the process of reflecting on my day and being grateful for certain things clears my head and prepares my brain for rest so it can recharge itself for the next day. Secondly, it extends my appreciation of things beyond just the people I know and the things that I'm comfortable with and allows me to appreciate elements that may be outside of my social circle, my work, the environment I've been in or the things I've seen and heard. And thirdly, my attitude has improved as I've adopted gratitude.

Studies show that when we write regularly about the things we are grateful for we train our brains to notice positive experiences, which increases our capacity to be more positive.[14] Studies also show that writing down on a regular basis what we are thankful for benefits our mood and coping behaviours, as well as our physical health.[15]

## Write a letter of gratitude

You can make yourself happier and nurture your relationship with another person by writing a thank you letter expressing your appreciation for that person's impact on your life. It doesn't have to be long — some of the best gratitude letters are short and to the point — but what it does need is meaning. By doing this unexpectedly, your level of gratitude will increase, as should the receiver's, and it will probably be one of the best surprises they will ever receive. Associate Professor Steve Toepfer's research looked directly at gratitude exercises and found that writing a thank you note or expressing gratitude to someone in a written form enhanced levels of satisfaction and happiness, as well as decreased symptoms of depression.[16] You can do it the traditional way, by handwriting a letter and sending it in the mail, or by email; or for the best impact you can write it out and deliver it yourself. That way, you can witness the receiver's response, which the research shows further increases your own appreciation and gratitude.[17] Ultimately, though, it really doesn't matter how you do it but from my experience a gratitude letter will be read many times over and is one of the most moving gratitude tools available to us.

Here are some suggestions for how to structure a gratitude letter. After the salutation, start by thanking the person. Be explicit in your detail and gratitude:

+ 'Thank you so much for …'
+ 'I am extremely grateful for …'
+ 'Without your support I …'
+ 'You have made such a difference to …'

Then give examples of what they have done:
+ 'Your help has enabled me to …'
+ 'I could not be the person I am without …'
+ 'You have added much value to …'
+ 'I appreciate your thinking and teamwork, which has …'

Then note your appreciation for them one more time:
+ 'Your support simply shows how important …'
+ 'You are my best friend and I love the fact that …'
+ 'Your leadership clearly shows that …'
+ 'I'm indebted to you for the …'

In closing, think about the relationship you have with the recipient and how you want to finish the letter.

## Gratitude walk

When stressed or feeling under pressure, a good way of clearing your mind and taking the tension out of your body is to go for a gratitude walk. This combines two key tools, just as we did with meditation. However, with a gratitude walk we are using exercise and gratitude together to combat the stress we are feeling and increase our levels of wellbeing. Walking is good for you. It can reduce the risk of heart disease and stroke while supporting better blood pressure, cholesterol, diabetes and muscle stiffness. It increases endorphins that decrease stress and lethargy while creating better blood circulation in the body.

Author Cheryl Rickman writes that by coupling walking with a grateful state of mind, you are bound to nurture a positive mind and body.[18] Rickman states that the goal of a gratitude walk is to observe the things you see around you as you walk. In other words, take it all in, be curious and aware of your surroundings, what buildings are you passing, what type of trees are there, if you can you see animals and if so what are they. Try to really listen to the sounds around you and identify what they are, and notice your movement — if you are you walking fast can you slow down? Is the earth underfoot flat or uneven? Are you on grass or concrete, and can you feel your feet connecting with the ground with each step?

The effects can be better if you can share a gratitude walk with a friend and experience together what is happening for each of you in that present moment.

## Morning tea or coffee gratitude

Many people start their day with a cup of tea or coffee, or a freshly squeezed juice. This ritual can be both pleasant and comforting, and for those people who find it difficult to consistently find the time or a way to remember to think about giving thanks, tying in a gratitude session with your morning cuppa is a simple and practical way to remember.

Once you have your drink, a good way to start your practice is to place both hands around your cup and hold it up close to your face. Straight away you might feel gratitude for either the warmth of the cup with its hot tea or coffee inside, or for the coolness of the cup with its contents of juice. Before having your first sip, take a deep breath of its contents and be grateful for its aroma, then take a sip and hold it in your mouth for a few seconds before swallowing. Feel the sensation of either the hot or cool fluid rolling over your taste buds then sliding down your throat. Take in the quiet of the morning or think about the beginning of a new day and its potential. This exercise allows you to start the day by choosing the right thoughts for you, just as you would choose the right clothes to wear that day.

I'm not a coffee or a tea drinker but I do enjoy a cup of hot chocolate. Whenever I have one I always have a ritual of placing my hands around the cup to feel its warmth on the palms of my hands, looking at the thickness of the froth with its chocolate-coated covering then placing the cup up to my lips so that I can smell the melted chocolate. This allows me to not only savour the moment and therefore make it more enjoyable and memorable, but also to be grateful for what I have right at that moment, all of which puts me in a positive frame of mind.

## Gratitude smile

For those people who feel they are very busy and don't have much free time to practice being grateful, this exercise can be done in under a minute.

Author Kristi Ling recommends that you practice the three Ss: smile, say thanks and set an intention. Ling states that this process is especially helpful if you want to ward off sudden bouts of tension by consciously smiling, as holding a smile for longer than seventeen seconds can alter the brain's chemistry and trigger happy feelings.[19] While you are smiling, think about adding the second S to the process —saying thanks — by thinking about something you are grateful for, such as your partner or a family member, your health, certain foods, your pet or the work you do. Then finally add the third S and set an intention to do something positive, such as thanking a colleague, going for a walk or listening to music and note how you feel once you have completed this goal.

## Meditation

By combining meditation and gratitude you are utilizing two of the most significant tools at our disposal that impact both our happiness and overall wellbeing at the same time.

As mentioned in Chapter 4, being mindful through mediation takes time and practice in order to broaden our thinking and build our personal resources. Meditation isn't always easy, especially if life is busy and we have competing deadlines and pressures from work, family and social commitments. Our mind can continually wonder and be distracted as it competes with the priority list of thoughts and to-do lists that reside within our brain. But as previously mentioned, if you can practise meditation (even by starting out slowly), then you can experience the wonderful benefits of gratitude, happiness and joy.

With meditation we spoke about the importance of being comfortable, relaxing your body, clearing your mind (and if you get distracted, acknowledging the distraction then letting it go so you can clear you mind again) and intentionally being aware of your breathing. The same principles apply when combining meditation with gratitude, the only difference being that instead of clearing your mind you visualize things you are grateful for. You may want to focus on being grateful for family members or friends, the roof above you head and the food on you table, or even things that we may take for granted, like the use of our senses. By practising gratitude meditation you can magnify your appreciation of the things that are part of your life on a regular basis, which builds a stronger contentment for what you have and how you live your life.

## Gratitude jar

This simple but effective exercise is a great one for both adults and children. First, get yourself any old jar and decorate it with a colourful label or maybe even paint the whole jar. By making a label or painting it, you create a special purpose for the jar and therefore help to remind yourself about gratitude. Place the jar in a prominent position in your house so that you will see it at least twice a day. This could be in your kitchen near your fridge, by your bedside or even in your bathroom next to your toothbrush. Every now and then, place some money in the jar and when the jar is full donate the contents to your favourite charity to help others. Placing it somewhere you can see it on a regular basis will help remind you that you have much to be grateful for in your life. Building this practice should enhance your overall happiness and wellbeing.

---

This chapter has looked at what gratitude is — the quality of being thankful, the readiness to show appreciation for, and to return, kindness — and at how practising gratitude, no matter what your inherent or current level of gratitude, can increase your overall health and wellbeing. We can look at gratitude in different ways, whether considering the past and being thankful for positive moments; whether focusing on the present and appreciating what we have now and not taking it for granted; or whether thinking about the future and being optimistic and hopeful in our attitude for things yet to come.

In his research into gratitude, Dr Robert Emmons of the University of California has discovered that gratitude is closely linked with attitude and that people who view life as important and consciously acquire an 'attitude of gratitude' will experience multiple levels of meaning and wellbeing in their lives. Emmons found that gratitude improves emotional and physical health and can strengthen relationships and communities. Though not easily acquired, gratitude is best attained by practising simple exercises that work for you and can be done on a regular basis, as without gratitude, Emmons writes, 'life can be lonely, depressing and impoverished'.[20] However, gratitude is more than just a positive emotion and the more you can cultivate it to broaden your thinking and build your personal resources the more it will energize, inspire and transform you while improving your health.

With this in mind, you might now like to take five minutes to complete the following Gratitude Inventory by answering a number of multiple choice questions to see how you score and how the key points listed at the end of this chapter can support you in building a stronger, more mindful thinking style.

## Gratitude Inventory

The purpose of this short questionnaire is to provide you with an opportunity to gain an insight into how gratitude may be playing out for you. While the questionnaire is built with best-practice frameworks, it is not designed to be a valid scientific reflection.

Take care in the way you review your results; they are best used as a conversation piece to explore positive actions that can be taken to further orient yourself towards a more positive and flourishing approach to your personal and/or professional life.

Below are seven statements. To what degree are these statements like you? Please use the following scale to indicate how much like you each statement is.

+ Definitely not like me    = 1 point
+ Not much like me    = 2 points
+ Not really sure    = 3 points
+ Somewhat like me    = 4 points
+ Definitely like me    = 5 points

| Statement | Score |
|---|---|
| 1.  I have so much in life to be grateful for. | |
| 2.  I never have difficulty thinking of things for which I am grateful. | |
| 3.  Even when I am feeling down or disappointed, I can still write a long list of things I am thankful for. | |
| 4.  I hardly ever hold a grudge when someone hurts or upsets me. | |
| 5.  I never go more than a few days without thinking about things that I am grateful for. | |
| 6.  I find it very easy to tell people how much I appreciate them and what they mean to me. | |
| 7.  People who I appreciate would easily remember the last time I expressed my gratitude to them. | |
| Total | |

Insights to consider

Now tally up your score from the questionnaire.

## Higher score (25–35)

You tend to be very aware of the things in your life that give you joy and find it easy to express this. You may frequently look for opportunities to express this to yourself or to others. You may also find you can recover from setbacks more quickly when you take the time to reflect upon the things you are grateful for.

## Mid-range Score (16–24)

You may find that your sense of gratitude changes from time to time. There may be some things you can easily reflect upon while other things may be harder for you to feel grateful for. Reflecting upon what might affect your levels of gratitude could be useful for when you are feeling low.

## Lower score (5–15)

You might find it difficult to think about the things in your life that bring you joy. You might also find this even more difficult when you are feeling negative or experiencing a setback. You may also at times feel unable to respond positively to others who can easily recognize the things they are grateful for.

# To sum up

The key points and tools from this chapter for our ORANGES toolkit are:

+ Gratitude is more than just a positive emotion.
+ Building gratitude in our lives also makes us more resilient.
+ Gratitude improves our overall health and wellbeing, including improved sleep. It builds our self-esteem, builds our relationships, increases empathy and reduces aggression.
+ Gratitude is one of the most powerful antidotes to negative emotions and depression.
+ Gratitude connects us to something larger than ourselves, whether this is with other people, a god or higher power, or nature.
+ Take time to appreciate things — a job well done, a painting, a beautiful environment.
+ Give someone positive feedback every day.
+ Create a gratitude journal.
+ Design your own gratitude jar.
+ Take a gratitude walk
+ Remember the three Ss: smile, say thanks and set an intention.
+ Engage in a gratitude meditation.
+ Take time to have a gratitude cup of tea or coffee.
+ Express thanks when someone compliments you. Tell them how it makes you feel.

# 6

# Energy and Enjoyment

**Energy** (*noun*) The capacity for activity or the exertion of power.

**Enjoyment** (*noun*) The state of feeling pleasure and joy.

> Gentlemen, why don't you laugh? With the fearful strain
> that is upon me day and night, if I did not laugh I should
> die, and you need this medicine as much as I do.
>
> **Abraham Lincoln, during the Civil War**

All emotions have energy behind them. Enjoyment is a high-energy emotion that releases tension and creates an upward spiral of positivity. Maximizing the enjoyment in our life can lead to feeling healthier and happier.

Barbara Fredrickson and colleagues found that while negativity can raise your blood pressure, positivity can calm it down.[1] In other words, positivity can put the brakes on negativity. Positivity acts like a reset button and allows us to take stock of what is happening and readjust ourselves to move forward in a better frame of mind. High-energy emotions such as enjoyment, excitement, zest and enthusiasm shift our mood and our physiology fast, and one of the best ways to increase your energy levels is through laughter. Laughter is one of the quickest ways you can activate the healing effect of positive emotion. In 1971 William Fry first demonstrated that just a few minutes of laughter a day can increase the heart rate, improve blood pressure and oxygen consumption while working the muscles in your face and stomach, all of which reduces stress, builds our feelings of pleasure and joy, and improves overall wellbeing.[2]

It's hard to argue that laughing isn't infectious. I think we have all been in the position where someone's laughter has triggered our sense of humour and before we know it we are joining them in the laugh, even if we don't quite know what we are laughing about.

Laughter is a unique vocal signal that exercises the heart, relaxes muscles, improves blood flow and increases energy expenditure. It is produced by your chest muscles and diaphragm contracting and capturing the air in your lungs then shooting this out with such force that it vibrates your larynx to create a sound. A good laugh can involve your whole body, with fifteen muscles used in your face alone. The other great thing about laughter is that you get the same benefit from it whether it's been done in a voluntary capacity or in a contrived or fake manner. Research undertaken by Professor

Maciej Buchowski found that laughter increased energy levels and heart rate by up to 20 per cent above the resting rate of a person.[3] And although it's no match for exercise when it comes to weight management, laughing for up to ten minutes a day (it doesn't have to be ten consecutive minutes) can result in the body burning up to 40 calories or the amount of a small piece of chocolate. This might not sound like much but if you are able to have a good belly laugh each day it could equate to about 2 kilograms each year.

The other great news about laughter is that it can relieve tense situations and bring people closer together. Genuine smiles and laughter send signals to others that we are friendly, open and receptive. According to laughter researcher Robert Provine, laughter is a part of our social DNA, something that connects humans in a profound way. It knows no boundaries of age, language and race, and people are 30 per cent more likely to laugh in a social setting that when alone.[4]

Laughter also relives pain and stress. Robin Dunbar states that the act of laughing triggers endorphins (neurotransmitters produced by the pituitary gland and hypothalamus) within our body that give us more energy and a feeling of comfort. When patients where shown comedy videos, Dunbar found that they needed less pain medication and registered a greater sense of joy than patients who were shown a documentary.[5] Also, people who laughed more were found to have even higher pain thresholds. Dunbar's work also examined the two types of laughter called Duchenne and non–Duchenne. Duchenne laughter is the natural, relaxed laughter that is stimulus driven, when people see or hear something that they deem funny. It's the type of laughter that engages the zygomatic muscles around the corners of your mouth as well as the orbicularis oculi muscle, which raises the muscles around your checks and eyes. The nature of a Duchenne laugh is highly sociable and largely responsible for the contagious affect where other people are stimulated to laugh simply by hearing another laugh. Though having similar benefits, a non-Duchenne laugh or a fake laugh is context driven and unconnected to any emotional experience, such as the laughter from a salesperson trying to sell you something or from a talk show host trying to engage their guest. This laugh only involves the zygomatic muscles around your mouth, generally doesn't last as long as a Duchenne laugh and requires much more work by the chest muscles to force out the air in your lungs.

Some other significant research by Dr Lee Berk of Loma Linda University shows that laughter has lasting effects and that the physiological effects of a 60-minute session of watching something humorous can last anywhere between twelve to 24 hours depending on the individual.[6] This supports the notion that seeking positive experiences that make us laugh and smile can support our physiology and foster greater wellbeing. Further to this, in collaboration with Stanley Tan, a diabetes specialist at Oakcrest Health Research Institute in the United States, Berk researched the impact of laughter on individuals with diabetes which brings with it the risk of heart attack, blindness and other autoimmune and blood complications. This study found that mirthful laughter in people with diabetes raised good cholesterol, lowered inflammation and therefore may lower the risk of cardiovascular disease.[7] Dr Berk describes himself as a 'hard core medical clinician and scientist' who is fascinated with the power of positive emotions. Dr Berk says: 'The best clinicians understand that there is an intrinsic physiological intervention brought about by positive emotions such as mirthful laughter, optimism and hope. Lifestyle choices have significant impact on health and disease and these are choices which we and the patient exercise control relative to prevention and treatment.'[8]

# Laughter and stress

Another key finding from Berk and Tan's research showed that laughter positively affects hormones in the endocrine system, including cortisol, a hormone made by the adrenal glands.[9] While cortisol has benefits such as helping maintain blood pressure, immune function and the body's anti-inflammatory system, consistently high levels of cortisol, which can be brought about by stress, have negative effects on the body. Laughter plays a significant role in reducing cortisol, lowering blood pressure, reducing the risk of stroke or heart attack and improving your immune system by generating more disease-fighting cells. It also supports improved memory, the ability to process information and an increase in your overall intelligence.[10]

It's well known that not eating the right types of food and not exercising can lead to weight gain but there are other influences that can make losing weight more difficult. One of these is having high levels of cortisol due to chronic or elevated levels of stress, and laughter can help reduce these levels while also reducing your overall stress.

In another study, Berk discovered that mirthful laughter produces brainwaves similar to those achieved in a true state of meditation. This therefore allows the individual to integrate their mind and body to promote a greater wholeness, health and wellness.

'When there is mirthful laughter,' says Berk, 'it's as if the brain gets a workout because the gamma wave band is in sync with multiple other areas that are in the same 30–40 hertz frequency. This allows for the subjective feeling of being able to think more clearly and have more interactive thoughts. This is of great value to individuals who need or want to revisit, reorganize or rearrange various aspects of their lives or experiences, to make them feel whole or more focused.'

Berk went on to say that, 'Laughter may not only be good medicine for the health of your body but also a good medicine for your brain.'[11]

Laughter is the natural enemy of stress simply because they are physiological opposites; the dominance of one tends to overshadow the other. Stress impacts people differently, however our understanding of it shows that it creates disorder in our bodies and can lead to depression, lack of self-esteem and confidence, as well as nullifying innovative thinking and creativity. Symptoms of stress include a lack of motivation, fear of things going wrong, a lack of energy, physical tension and tiredness, not being able to feel moments of joy, not sleeping well, headaches, changes in eating habits and many others. Most people live with a little bit of stress on a regular basis but when this builds to a deep or chronic level then our body releases more cortisol, making you more susceptible to becoming ill, anxious and even more stressed.

Endocrinologist Hans Selye stated that laughter was a form of good stress known as 'eustress' — positive kind of stress that enhances our functioning and gives us positives feelings, which make us feel good about ourselves — and that laughter in stressful or painful situations can have significant benefits to our overall wellbeing.[12] An example of this would be laughing after someone or something has unexpectedly scared you, the thrill of watching a horror movie, completing a challenging or high-pressured task at work, the joy of childbirth or the experience of overcoming a fear of heights, flying or riding a rollercoaster. Laughter quickly reduces stress levels, provides enjoyment and helps create a new mental perspective that allows us to see problems or challenges once perceived as large as minor or even non-existent.

# Nature's energy pill

Author and humour expert Dr Paul McGhee states that 'anger and anxiety are energy sapping emotions'. His research has shown that living with anger, anxiety or fear on a daily or regular basis, whether it's at work or at home, changes the language we use and mentally, emotionally and physically depletes you while draining you of energy you need to be productive, satisfied and happy. His research, conducted over twenty years, outlines the many physical, mental and social benefits that laughter brings and show how laughter is nature's natural energy pill and antidote to the damaging effects of stress.[13] Quite simply, it enriches our bloodstream with loads of oxygen, which gives us the energy to tackle the emotions that may drain or deplete us. He says: 'Your sense of humour and laughter is one of the most powerful tools you have to make certain that your daily mood and emotional state support good health'.[14]

At work we introduced something called 'fun therapy' to start every meeting. This meant that all our meetings needed to start with something fun — a joke, an optimistic message or story, a game or activity. It could be long or short and was completely voluntary to participate in. It didn't take long before this quirky way of starting a meeting became the norm as people felt the individual and collective benefits of having fun and laughing. Our culture of positivity grew in part because of it, as creating fun before a meeting stimulated our people, got their brains activated and engaged and also relaxed and relieved tension. It bonded people and teams, it supported communication and improved energy and the language people used, all of which made the workplace a more productive, efficient and engaged place to work.

# Language

A simple but effective tool to help with monitoring your energy is to look at the language you use. By doing a positive reframe exercise we can train ourselves to accentuate the positive and eliminate the negative where appropriate.

Try to transform the following energy-sapping phrases into ones which emphasize what you can do and what 'good' looks like. Reframe them with positive language that is congruent with how you speak and therefore sounds authentically you. For example, you might change 'Let's not miss the deadline this time' to 'I'm confident that our preparation and planning will ensure that we will have it ready by the due date'.

Now read the statements below and rephrase them for yourself:

+ 'I'm tired, shattered, exhausted.'
+ 'Don't forget to …'
+ 'I'll never be able to do this.'
+ 'Don't hesitate to contact me.'
+ 'I don't know …'
+ 'That's not a bad idea.'
+ 'This is just hopeless.'
+ 'I always get nervous before making presentations or speaking in public.'
+ 'Don't worry too much about …'
+ 'Don't waste your time on doing that.'
+ 'This is going to be really difficult.'
+ 'I mustn't be late again.'
+ 'Sorry to bother you but I won't take up much of your time.'
+ 'Don't get me wrong, I'm not trying to criticize you but …'
+ 'Let's try to muddle our way through this.'
+ 'So, what exactly is your problem?'

# Energy and exercise

Another key tool to building energy is exercise. If you love playing sports or going for a run or walk, then you will know how great you feel after a game or workout. Even if you sometimes don't feel like doing some form of exercise, the findings are universal that you do feel better once you have done it. The research in this area clearly identifies the positive impact that exercise has on improved mood and mental wellbeing. Physical activity stimulates the release of chemicals in the brain called endorphins, which have a positive impact on your brain and body.[15] Other research states that exercise can clear the brain and act as a diversion from negative thoughts.[16] Exercise improves mood and adds to personal growth and goal attainment, which results from mastering a physical skill.[17] Further research has found that exercise that contains social interaction contributes to personal satisfaction and mood enhancement.[18]

Physical activity actively delivers oxygen and nutrients to your tissues and helps your cardiovascular system work more effectively. It can improve your muscle strength, boost your endurance and increase your overall levels of energy. In a study published in the *Psychological Bulletin*, researchers analysed 70 studies on exercise and fatigue that involved more than 6800 participants. The study revealed that people who previously had been inactive and then completed an exercise program improved their energy and strength levels in contrast to groups that did no exercise. The summary also found that over 90 per cent of these studies showed the same result.[19] Overwhelmingly, studies show the more you move the more energy and less fatigue you have. In fact, a study published in *Psychotherapy and Psychosomatics* reported that inactive people who normally complained of low energy and fatigue could increase levels of energy by 20 per cent and decrease fatigue by as much as 65 per cent by simply participating in low-intensity exercise.[20]

The explanation for this lies deep within the cellular level of our bodies. Here science has found mitochondria, tiny energy-producing organelles found in many cells of the body. As you move around, your body makes mitochondria to meet your energy needs. The more you move around the more you make, and the more mitochondria you have the greater the boost to your metabolism and the greater ability you have to produce more energy.

I know how much better I feel when I do some form of regular exercise. Whenever possible I aim to do regular exercise but at times, for whatever reason, I sometimes fall off the wagon. During these times, I ensure that I don't mentally beat myself up about it by understanding and accepting the reason why I'm not exercising, while at the same time putting forth a strategy to start again on a certain date when I'll have the time. However, when I am exercising I know I feel less fatigued, I'm a better decision-maker, I feel generally stronger and healthier, I handle stress and pressure better and my energy levels are higher.

---

This chapter has looked at what energy is — the capacity for activity, or the exertion of power — and enjoyment — the state of feeling pleasure and joy — and how all emotions have energy behind them. Feeling and thinking in a positive way allows us to be present in the current moment, to appreciate what is happening and, if necessary, readjust ourselves to move forward in a better frame of mind. If negativity can spike our levels of stress and blood pressure, then high-energy emotions such as enjoyment, excitement, zest and enthusiasm can calm it down and laughter is one of the quickest ways you can activate a high-energy emotion.

We all know how wonderful laughter makes us feel. It triggers a positive physical response and change within our bodies, strengthens our immune system, boosts our energy levels and protects us from stress and pain. Added to this, shared laughter brings people together, creates social engagement and increases happiness. And the best news about all of this is that laughter is free. If you use laughter as a tool it will support you in broadening your thinking and building your personal resources.

With this in mind you may now like to take five minutes and complete the following Energy and Enjoyment Inventory by answering a number of multiple choice questions to see how you score and how the key points listed at the end of this chapter can support you in building your high-energy emotions to create greater levels of enjoyment and energy.

## Energy and Enjoyment Inventory

The purpose of this short questionnaire is to provide you with an opportunity to gain an insight into how your energy may be playing out for you. While the questionnaire is built with best-practice frameworks, it is not designed to be a valid scientific reflection.

Take care in the way you review your results; they are best used as a conversation piece to explore positive actions that can be taken to further orient yourself towards a more positive and flourishing approach to your personal and/or professional life.

Below are seven statements. To what degree are these statements like you? Please use the following scale to indicate how much like you each statement is.

+ Definitely not like me    = 1 point
+ Not much like me    = 2 points
+ Not really sure    = 3 points
+ Somewhat like me    = 4 points
+ Definitely like me    = 5 points

| Statement | Score |
|---|---|
| 1. I am very aware of what upsets me. | |
| 2. I am very aware of how my feelings influence the way I interact with others. | |
| 3. I pick up on my change of mood quickly after it develops. | |
| 4. I am very aware of the things that energize me. | |
| 5. I often engage in activities that make me feel positive. | |
| 6. I demonstrate positive moods and emotions often. | |
| 7. I can quickly adjust to my own and others' negative moods to help create more positivity. | |
| Total | |

Insights to consider

Now tally up your score from the questionnaire.

### Higher score (25–35)

You may more easily recognize those things that create both positive and negative emotions for you. You may also be able to more easily and deliberately do things that help you adjust quickly and create greater amounts of positivity. You may also experience a higher ratio of positive emotions to negative emotions most days.

### Mid-range Score (16–24)

While your mood is stable most of the time, you may find that cultivating positive emotion is easier at times than at others. Exploring what might make it easier or more difficult to cultivate positive emotions could be useful for when you are facing challenges.

### Lower score (5–15)

You may tend to take a while to notice what mood you are in and how your behaviour has been affected by that mood. You might also find it more difficult to deliberately engage in activities that will help you shift into a more positive mood. Even when you want to give yourself a lift you might find it more difficult to think of things that energize you.

# To sum up

The key points and tools from this chapter for our ORANGES toolkit are:

+ Laughter releases a cocktail of chemicals in the body that boost the immune system, particularly in areas related to anti-viral and anti-tumour defences. It boosts the secretion of growth hormones, which enhances our key immune responses, and reduces the secretion of cortisol. Laughter increases energy expenditure and heart rate by up to 20 per cent. It releases endorphins that boost self-confidence, optimism, feelings of self-worth and act as a natural pain killer.

+ Laughter stimulates blood flow and circulation, and aids in relaxing our muscles.

+ The positive effects of watching something funny for 60 minutes can last anywhere between twelve to 24 hours.

+ Laughter strengthens social bonds and relationships, and enhances teamwork.

+ All emotions have energy behind them.

+ Practise your positive reframes.

+ We can increase or decrease the energy of our emotions when we choose.

+ Exercise — play sport, jog or go for a walk. The main thing is to get moving.

+ Do things that make you smile, or watch something funny to help create positive, high-energy emotions.

# 7

## Strengths

**Strengths** (*noun*) A pre-existing capacity for a way of behaving, thinking or feeling that allows us to perform at our best.

> Now is no time to think of what you do not have. Think of what you can do with what there is.
>
> **Ernest Hemmingway**

Strengths are the genuine and authentic resources we have that allow us to perform at our best. When we use our strengths, we enjoy what we are doing, we do it effortlessly and we feel that we are working towards fulfilling our potential. When we are doing something we love and we are doing it well, our strengths provide us with the capacity to excel. In using our strengths we can often feel a sense of authenticity, motivation, control, zest and exhilaration. Strengths also give us energy, they give you a high or a reverberation that makes you feel as if you're experiencing the real you.

Leading positive psychology and strengths expert Alex Linley defines strengths as a 'pre-existing capacity for a particular way of behaving, thinking or feeling that is authentic and energizing to the user, and enables optimal functioning, developing and performance'.[1] Some examples of strengths include courage, creativity, curiosity, gratitude, humour, mission, optimism, resilience, resolve and strategic awareness among many others. While personality is the summary of our entire psychological make-up, strengths are the positive components — what's best in you.

Research shows that when people use their strengths they feel happier and more confident, are less stressed, more resilient and optimistic in their thinking, more grateful and are more engaged in their self-development.[2] Studies also reveal that when we combine our strengths with others and assist them to use theirs, we create the capacity to build stronger and more co-operative relationships, enabling greater collaboration and harmony.[3] As Linley states: 'Using our strengths is the smallest thing we can do to make the biggest difference' at home, work or in the community.[4]

One of the early pioneers of the positive psychology movement, Dr Martin Seligman, has found that people are less stressed, more energized, engaged and have an overall greater feeling of wellbeing when they use their strengths in a new and different way on a regular basis.[5] By using their strengths people are more likely to achieve their goals, be efficient, successful and more effective.

# Understanding your personal strengths

Seligman and his colleague Chris Peterson have developed a questionnaire called VIA (Values in Action) Signature Strengths to help individuals identify their strengths. It examines 24 character strengths within six categories, called virtues. It's a free program and is universally recognized as a questionnaire that fits across any culture around the world. (See https://www.authentichappiness.sas.upenn.edu/)

Understanding your strengths is more than just thinking about what you are good at. For a strength to really blossom some essential ingredients are required, and given that according to Linley's research only one in three people fully understand their strengths, it's no wonder that the majority of people miss what strengths are really about and what they can do for them.

The two key elements of strengths are defined by the presence of performance and energy. In other words, you are doing whatever it is you are doing at a high-performance level and experiencing a sense of energy while doing it. Whether you've gotten up early in the morning eager to take on a task at home, undertaken a creative activity like painting or music, embedded yourself into a project at work or even trained and prepared yourself for a physical challenge, we have all had that feeling of being in the zone and feeling like this was what we were meant to do.

Linley and his colleagues have developed a leading-edge assessment tool called Realise2 which you can use to gain an understanding of your strengths and the energy that underpins them (see https://realise2.cappeu.com/4/login_public.asp). This tool can be extremely supportive in a work environment where you are looking to maximize the skills and talents of your people while understanding what activities de-energize them. The assesment provides tools that will help you to discover the difference between the strengths that come naturally and energize you and those strengths that de-energize you or you simply don't use very often. The tool looks at 60 individual strengths that sit within four categories, and are underpinned by three dimensions:

+ performance — how good you are at doing the activity
+ energy — how energizing you find the activity
+ use — how often you actually do the activity.

The four strength categories are:

+ Realized strengths: strengths that you use well on a regular basis and that energize you. These are your strongest strengths and a very powerful resource. The more you get to know these strengths, the more you will understand how to marshal and combine them when appropriate to achieve greater performance and outcomes.

+ Learned behaviours: strengths that you have learned and perform well when using them, but they de-energize you. These pose a potential risk for you as they will impact your levels of energy and wellbeing. If not used in moderation, they will over time lead to burn-out. The aim is to moderate the use of these strengths or stop using them if possible. When you do need to use them, then aim to 'sandwich' a realized strength on either side to ensure that you enter and leave the activity with an energizing strength.

+ Weakness: traits that might be strengths in others, but which you use poorly and that de-energize you. If your weaknesses are casing you some concern, look for ways to minimize their use and impact. Use these strengths as little as possible or only when necessary, and if necessary look for someone who has a strength that will complement and support your weakness.

+ Unrealized strengths: strengths you don't use often but when used you use well. Look for opportunities to introduce these more often into your daily life. The more you develop these strengths, the more varied your learning will become.[6]

## Utilizing your strengths

Once you have established what your strengths are and have an understanding of the roles they play in your life, there are four key activities you should aim to achieve:

+ Marshal your realized strengths for best performance.
+ Moderate your learned behaviours for viable performance.
+ Minimize your weaknesses to make them irrelevant.
+ Maximize your unrealized strengths to support growth and development.

To help support the above, and to get the most out of your strengths, try to do the following:

+ Combine strengths where possible to maximise their impact.
+ Experiment. Look for tasks at work or home to which you could apply some of your unrealized strengths. The more you practise with these strengths, the more chance that they will develop into a strength that just comes naturally to you.
+ Challenge. As your strengths toolkit develops and expands, look for opportunities to apply your strengths to new and challenging situations.
+ Monitor. As you develop, grow and expand your strengths, always evaluate the effectiveness of their use with the situation at hand. Your own observations and feedback will support your efforts to broaden your thinking and build your personal resources.

At work we used a strengths-based program to great effect. In one situation, we were able to identify a strength in a person whose current role didn't require her to use that strength. Every day this staff member would be out in the community delivering services and talking to our stakeholders to ensure we were meeting their needs. We discovered and identified that she had a wonderful skill for detail, and in particular proofreading, which led her to become our go-to person to review all our important communication pieces before they went to print or were placed on a web page. By giving her time within her current role to do this, we utilized a skill previously unknown to us and in turn created a higher level of engagement, as she was not only utilizing a strength she loved to use (and that made her feel good) but her workplace was also acknowledging this and allowing her to use it beyond her normal job.

It's important to acknowledge that we can't all be good at everything, and that strengths and weaknesses lie within us all. Even the world's most successful people have weaknesses, yet over time they have learnt to minimize these, to seek support from people around them to complement their weaknesses and to focus on maximizing their strengths.

## Practise to improve your strengths

The best way to develop and improve your strengths is simply through practice and regular use. Remember: forming a new habit takes practice and you can train your strengths to be just that — a good habit.

American-based Arthur Rubinstein was regarded as one of the greatest pianists of the 20th century. He used his strengths of adventure (was prepared to take risks when playing his music), ability to remain centred (an inner composure and self- assurance that he could improve) and detail (focusing on the small things that others may miss) to practise as much as twelve hours a day in his quest to be the best. He knew that to be the best he had to create a habit of playing, so his technique could transmit the joy of music through a natural, unforced and unflurried style that gave him world recognition. He said that if he missed practice for one day, then he knew it. But if he missed practice for three days, then his audience knew it.[7] We all might not want to be the best in the world at something, however we all have strengths and natural abilities that, if practised and honed, can energize us, propel us forward and become a natural habit.

## How to spot strengths

Most people have an understanding of their strengths, but for those who are unsure or for those who may know their strengths but not those of others, Linley has developed some strengths-spotting tips that will allow you to know what you are looking for and to get the most from your strengths. In order to make the best use of your strengths you need to know what to look for, so start paying attention to the things that you and other people do well, how you or they talk about them and what energy levels you or they show. See how many strengths you can spot in the people around you through your normal daily activities.

The ten tips for spotting strengths are:

+ **Childhood memories.** What did you do well as a child that you still do well today but possibly better? Strengths often have a deep connection to our childhood.
+ **Energy.** What tasks or activities make you feel alive and active when you are doing them? These are very likely your strengths.
+ **Authenticity.** When do you feel genuine? It is at these times when you will be using your strengths in some way.

+ **Ease.** When things come instinctively to you and you perform them well, then you will be using your strengths.

+ **Attention.** When you are focused and are able to not be distracted then you more than likely paying attention to the things that align with your strengths.

+ **Rapid learning.** When we pick up things quickly and naturally this indicates that we are aligning with our strengths.

+ **Motivation.** Things that we enjoy doing and that energize us are aligned with our strengths.

+ **Voice.** When we talk with passion, excitement and energy, we are often talking about our strengths.

+ **Words and phrases.** Listen to the language and phrases you use. When you are saying, 'I'm excited to ...' or 'How good is ...', the chances are it's a strength to which you are referring.

+ **To-do lists.** Notice the things that often get done first on your to-do list. This reveals the things we like to do and relates to our strengths.[8]

---

This chapter has looked at what strengths are and how when people recognize and use their strengths they perform better, achieve results faster, feel more resilient, energized, satisfied and engaged.

By understanding your strengths you can better prepare yourself for greater communications, interactions and relationships at home and in the workplace. You can develop a style that allows you to be authentic and perform at your personal and professional best. Recognizing and understanding strengths in others increases collaboration, communication and connection. Knowing others' strengths allows you to leverage and maximize these for a common goal or objective that will be more productive and efficient for all concerned.

Addressing the four areas mentioned earlier — marshalling your strengths, moderating your learned behaviours, minimizing your weaknesses or maximizing your unrealized strengths — will allow you to optimize your potential and enjoy life from a more positive perspective. With this information you can be more in touch with your needs, values and what you want to get out of life. You can then plan the direction you want to go in and participate in things that energize and allow you to perform at a higher level on a more regular basis. Strengths help build resilience and can assist you in challenging or difficult times, by allowing you to accept your feelings, remain focused and look towards using new and current strengths as the foundation stones on which to move forward. By combining, experimenting, challenging and monitoring your strengths you can increase the tools in your toolkit by broadening your thinking and building your personal resources.

With this in mind you may now like to take five minutes and complete the following Strengths Inventory by answering a number of multiple choice questions to see how you score and how the key points listed at the end of this chapter can support you in identifying your strengths to create greater levels of enjoyment and energy.

### Strengths inventory

The purpose of this short questionnaire is to provide you with an opportunity to gain an insight into how your strengths may be playing out for you. While the questionnaire is built with best-practice frameworks, it is not designed to be a valid scientific reflection.

Take care in the way you review your results; they are best used as a conversation piece to explore positive actions that can be taken to further orient yourself towards a more positive and flourishing approach to your personal and/or professional life.

Below are seven statements. To what degree are these statements like you? Please use the following scale to indicate how much like you each statement is.

+ Definitely not like me     = 1 point
+ Not much like me         = 2 points
+ Not really sure           = 3 points
+ Somewhat like me       = 4 points
+ Definitely like me         = 5 points

| Statement | Score |
|---|---|
| 1. I can easily name the top three strengths that I have and use often. | |
| 2. I can easily name the top three strengths of friends, family and co-workers. | |
| 3. I know how to create opportunities for myself to play to my strengths on a daily basis. | |
| 4. I find out other people's strengths as quickly as I can. | |
| 5. I always look for opportunities to help other people play to their strengths. | |
| 6. People I work with would easily remember the last time I recognized one of their strengths at play. | |
| 7. I don't believe there is such a thing as a person without any strengths. | |
| Total | |

Now tally up your score from the questionnaire.

**Higher score (25–35)**

You may tend to know your strengths well and know how to create opportunities to play to them often. You may be more likely to praise others than to criticize them. You may also be more likely to get more out of yourself and others because of this approach.

**Mid-range score (16–24)**

You may be using some of your strengths without realizing. You may also at times tap into others' strengths without doing it deliberately. Paying more deliberate attention to how you are using your own or recognising others' strengths may enable you to get even more out of yourself and others.

**Lower score (5–15)**

You may find that you tend to get de-energized quickly when doing tasks that don't play to your strengths. You may also tend to find fault more often and do more criticizing than praising of others. You might find it difficult to recognize others' strengths and create an environment where you and others can use your strengths more often.

# To sum up

The key points and tools from this chapter for our ORANGES toolkit are:

+ The two key elements of strengths are the presence of performance and energy. In other words, you are doing whatever it is you are doing at a high-performance level and experiencing a sense of energy while doing it.
+ Learn how to spot strengths in yourself and others using the ten tips for spotting strengths.
+ Marshal your realized strengths for best performance.
+ Moderate your learned behaviours for sustainable performance.
+ Minimize your weaknesses and, if possible, make them irrelevant.
+ Maximize your unrealized strengths to support growth and development.
+ Using strengths will greatly support you in achieving your goals and objectives.
+ Maximizing your strengths allows you higher engagement, greater mindfulness and less stress.
+ Knowing your strengths supports the building of resilience.
+ Greater confidence, self-esteem, zest and vitality are more evident the more people use their strengths.

# Postscript

The organization I talked about at the start of this book is an Australian national children's cancer organization called Camp Quality. When I took on the role as CEO I knew things weren't right within the organization and it was facing some major difficulties from a people, financial and business perspective.

The impetus for change within the people and the organization as a whole was real. After many prosperous years, the wheels had fallen off as the organization and its people accepted bad business habits that created a cancerous culture. The culture fed on negativity and a failure to invest in its people or its values.

The organization had recently gone through some very tough times: a revenue project to raise much-needed funds was a financial disaster that had at the time crippled the organization, and everywhere you looked there was low morale (a number of staff were receiving counselling due to stress and anxiety). There was reduced revenue, increased costs, little accountability, change-averse behaviours, declining participation of our stakeholders and governance practices that were endangering the safety of the children we were there to care for and support. The government had given cause to the organization that its licence to operate was going to be revoked and the threat to our very existence was real. The overall wellbeing of our people was poor and many were generally not happy, nor open to any form of change. Within those early days my brief was very clear — firstly to plug the holes to stop the ship from sinking and, once that was achieved, look at how to make our people feel better.

Despite the doom and gloom that surrounded everyone in those days there were signs of hope. This was particularly evident in the children and families that we supported, who were dealing with a life impacted by cancer. To see families' lives turned upside down by the news of their child's diagnosis was heart wrenching, but to also see their amazing attitude, resilience and optimism was inspiring. The determination of our families to make good of a bad situation, to focus on what they could control, live in the moment, never give up and share their strengths with others was the catalyst for us to change the way we thought, acted and behaved as individuals. They not only tackled a bad situation from a positive perspective, they wanted to understand how to mentally and emotionally develop psychological skills that would stop other potential problems from developing.

In a world where clinical psychology devotes time and resources to fixing people's problems through researching and applying psychological theories, positive psychology is concerned with researching and applying the effects of positive thoughts and emotions on people's general wellbeing. This then ensures they can focus on their strengths, understand their emotions and have tools that build resilience and optimistic behaviours, which in turn enables them to be better equipped to bounce back from challenges and adversities. It complements clinical psychology and other traditional areas by focusing not just on problems but also on how to prevent problems developing in the first place.

Our families were living proof of the benefits of positive thoughts and emotions, and how having some of these skills gave them the capacity to broaden their thinking and build their personal resources. Seeing how they dealt with the stresses, challenges and uncertainty that life could bring and do it with a positive attitude, humour, gratitude and optimism was something we could all learn from.

By taking the lead from how our families dealt with adversity, ORANGES was designed to provide specific skills that assisted people to build positive emotions, boost personal resilience, advance mindfulness, enhance relationships and encourage a healthy, fulfilling and grateful lifestyle. Over time, our ORANGES program was rolled out within the organization with great effect and from that Camp Quality and its people have seen enormous changes from an emotional, mental and physical perspective, positively impacting the wellbeing of our individuals, teams and the whole organization. It is no coincidence that the tagline under the Camp Quality logo states 'Laughter is the best medicine'. The business metrics improved, with an increase in revenue, business partnerships, staff and volunteers. Most importantly we increased the support and services to children with cancer. Along the way we won numerous organizational awards for our transparency, marketing, innovation, partnerships and staff engagement. We set the benchmark for child protection policies, procedures and practices and have consistently been voted in the top ten of Australia's most trusted charities.

The next step of course is up to you. No doubt there will be some people who will jump into ORANGES and give it a go, while others will dip their toe in the water and try a few things, and some might resist or feel they don't need to improve. Whatever your choice, ORANGES is not a spectator sport; you will need to be involved and be willing to participate. Your wellbeing is your choice and you can choose to search the world for the negatives or you can choose to search the world for the things that make you happier and more fulfilled, and that have meaning for you. If you do decide that is what you would like then you can train your brain to carry emotional, physical and mental skills which encourage a healthier lifestyle.

Regardless of where you sit, the main thing is that this is a living and breathing program that has worked for thousands of people who have been impacted by Camp Quality. It is not something made up from marketing wizardry, nor does it come directly off a shelf with no proven track record. ORANGES is alive and well and continues to improve the lives of people facing the enormous challenges that cancer brings. The people at Camp Quality are not unlike you or I, they have no special powers — they are simply ordinary human beings. It is, however, the choices they make that are extraordinary. If these people can live in a way that you want to, then what is stopping you from making the choice to live that way as well?

# Acknowledgments

This book would not have been possible without the support of so many people who have guided, motivated, energized, frustrated, encouraged, questioned and challenged me. Whether directly or indirectly I have learnt much about life from the following people who in some way have all inspired me, left their mark on me and made me a better person. In no particular order my heartfelt thanks goes to Katie Prager, Michael Crossland, Vanessa Rider, Vivien Sonego, Bob Alexander, Tegan Davies, Sue Langley, Peter Kite, Renata Consiglio, Deborah Cox, Ken Moffat, James O'Toole, Mel Neil, John Foote, Anne Sutton, Margot Grant and all the staff, volunteers and families (past and present) of Camp Quality. Thanks to everyone at Exisle especially Gareth for his faith, Anouska for her patience and Karen for her amazing eye for detail.

And finally thanks to my family (Jo, Mia and Oliver) for their support, love and keeping me fed as I spent hours locked away in the back room, typing away with my two fingers.

# Endnotes

## Introduction

1. Dean, J. 2013, *Making Habits Breaking Habits*, One World Publications, 2013, London, p. 7.

2. Barsade, S.G. and Gibson, D.E. 2007, 'Why does effect matter in organisations?' *Academy of Management Perspectives*, 21 (1), pp. 36–59.

3. Fredrickson, B. and Branigan, C. 2005, 'Positive emotions broaden the scope of attention and thought action repertoires', *American Psychologist*, 56 (3), pp. 218–26.

4. Lemonick, M.D. 2005, 'The biology of joy: Scientists know plenty about depression, now they are starting to understand the roots of positive emotion', *Time*, vol. 165, 3, p. 12.

5. Biswas-Diener, R. and Dean B. 2007, 'Positive psychology coaching: Putting the science of happiness to work for your clients', *Journal of Positive Psychology*, vol. 4, issue 5, pp. 426–9.

6. Zelman, D.C., Howland, E.W., Nichols S. N., and Cleeland, C.S. 1991, 'The effects of induced mood on laboratory pain', *Pain*, vol. 46, (1), pp. 105–11.

7. Harter, J.K., Schmidt, F.L. and Keyes, C. 2003, 'Wellbeing in the workplace and

its relationship to business outcomes', in Haidt, J. and Keyes, C. (eds) *Flourishing: The positive person and the good life*, American Psychological Association, Washington DC, pp. 205–24.

## What makes ORANGES different?

1. Fredrickson, B. 'Positive emotions transforms us', YouTube video, 21 June 2011.

2. Lyubomirsky, S., King, L., and Diener, E. 2005.

3. Barsade, S.G. and Gibson, D.E. 2007.

4. Lemonick, M.D. 2005.

5. ibid.

6. Vitaliano, P.P., Scanlon, J.M., Ochs H.D., Syrjala, K., Siegler, I.C and Snyder, E.A. 1998.

7. Lyubomirsky, S., King, L., and Diener, E. 2005.

8. Barsade, S.G. and Gibson, D.E. 2007.

9. Epstein, R. 2009, 'The science of creativity', *Grad PSYCH Magazine*, American Psychological Association, p. 14.

10. Zelman, D.C., Howland, E.W., Nicholas, S.N., and Cleeland, C.S. 1991, 'The effects of induced mood on laboratory pain', Pain, 46(1), pp. 105–11.

11. Lemonick, M.D. 2005.

12. Danner, D.D., Snowdon, D.A. and Friesen, W.V. 2001, 'Positive emotions in early life and longevity: Findings from the nun study', *Journal of Personality and Social Psychology*, vol. 80, (5), pp. 804–13.

13. Frey, B.S. 2011, 'Happy people live longer', *Science*, pp. 331, 542.

14. Thoits, P.A. and Hewitt, L.N. 2001, 'Volunteer work and wellbeing', *Journal of Health and Social Behavior*, vol. 42, no. 2, pp. 115–31.

15. Lyubomirsky, S., King, L., and Diener, E. 2005.

16. Harter, J.K., Schmidt, F.L. and Keyes, C. 2003.

17. Lyubomirsky, S., King, L., and Diener, E. 2005.

18. ibid.


# 1: Optimism

1.  Danner, D.D., Snowden, D.A., and Friesen, W.V. 2001, 'Positive emotions in early life and longevity: Findings from a nun study', *Journal of Persona and Social Psychology*, vol. 80 (5), pp. 804–13.


# 2: Resilience

1.  Reivich, K. And Shatte, A. 2003, *The Resilience Factor: 7 keys to finding your inner strength and overcoming life's hurdles*, Broadway Books, New York.

2.  Brown, B, 'Joy is the most vulnerable emotion', *Huffington Post*, 18 October 2013.

3.  Reivich, K. And Shatte, A. 2003, *The Resilience Factor: 7 keys to finding your inner strength and overcoming life's hurdles*, Broadway Books, New York, p. 3.

4.  Reivich, K. and Shatte, A. 2003, pp. 96–115.

5.  Duckworth, A. 2016, *Grit: The power of passion and perseverance*, Scribner Book Company, New York.

6.  ibid.

7.  Fredrickson, B. et al., 2003, 'What good are positive emotions in crises? A prospective study of resilience and emotions following the terrorist attacks on the United States on September 11, 2001', *J. Pers Soc Psychol*, 84(2), pp. 365–76.


# 3: Attitude

1.  Frankl, V.E. 1946, *Man's Search for Meaning*, Random House, London.

2.  Lyubomirsky, S. 2008, *The How of Happiness: A new approach to getting the life you want*, Piatkus, London.

3. Billing, J.P. and Hershberger, S.L et al., 1996, 'Life events and personality in late adolescence, genetic and environmental relations', *Genetics*, 26(6), pp. 543–54.

4. Dwek, C. S. 2007, *Mindset: The new psychology of success*, Ballantine Books, New York.

## 4: Now

1. Langer, E.J. 2014, *The Art of Noticing: Research on mindlessness and mindfulness*, The Langer Mindfulness Institute, Cambridge, Mass.

2. Forrester, M. 2012, 'Breaking study is the first to show link between being present in the moment and ageless DNA', accessed at www.wakingtimes.com

3. Killingsworth, M. 2011, Ted Talk (Cambridge, Mass), accessed at www.ted.com/talks/matt_killingsworth

4. ibid.

5. Csikszentmihalyi, M. 1997, *Finding Flow: The psychology of engagement with everyday life*, Basic Books, New York.

6. ibid.

7. Kashdan, T.B., Rose, P. and Fincham, F.D. 2004, 'Curiosity and exploration', *Journal of Personality Assessment*, 82 (3), pp. 291–305.

8. Kashdan, T.B. 2009, *Curious: Discover the missing ingredient to a fulfilling life*, HarperCollins, New York.

9. Raine, A., Reynolds, C., Venables, P.H. and Mednick, S.A. 2002, 'Stimulation seeking and intelligence: A prospective longitudinal study', *Journal of Personality and Social Psychology*, vol. 82, no. 4, pp. 663–74.

10. Ranganath, C., Gruber, M.J. and Gelman, B. 2014, 'States of curiosity modulate hippocampus-dependent learning via the dopaminergic circuit', *Neuron*, vol. 84(2), pp. 486–96.

11. ibid.

12. Lyubomirsky, S., King, L. and Diener, E. 2005, 'The benefits of frequent positive affect: Does happiness lead to success?' *Psychological Bulletin*, 131(6), pp. 803–55.

13. Harker, L. and Keltner, D. 2001, 'Expressions of positive emotion in women's college yearbook pictures', *Journal of Personality and Social Psychology*, 80(1), pp. 112–24.

14. Gallup, 2014, Positive Experience Index, accessed at www.gallup.com

15. Lyubomirsky, S., King, L. and Diener, E. 2005.

## 5: Gratitude

1.   Thoits, P.A. and Hewitt, L.N. 2001.

2.   Vitaliano, P.P., Scanlon, J.M., Ochs, H.D., Syrjala, K., Siegler, I.C. and Snyder, E.A. 1998, 'Psychosocial stress moderates the relationship of cancer history with natural killer cell activity', *Annals of Behavioral Medicine*, 20, pp. 199–208.

3.   Emmons, R.A. and McCullough, M.E. 2004, *The Psychology of Gratitude*, Oxford Press, New York.

4.   ibid.

5.   Digdon, N. 2011, Effects of constructive worry, imagery distraction and gratitude interventions on sleep quality', *Applied Psychology Health and Wellbeing*, vol. 3, issue 2, pp. 127–227.

6.   Morin, A. 2014, 'Personality and individual differences', *Science Direct*, vol. 69, pp. 1–238.

7.   DeWall, N.C. Lambert N.M., Pond, R.S., Kashdan, T.B. and Fincham, F.D. 2012, 'Gratitude: A grateful heart is a nonviolent heart', *Society for Personality and Social Psychology*, 3(2), pp. 232–40.

8.   Aloge, S.B., Haidt, J. and Gable, S.L. 2008, 'Gratitude and relationships in everyday life', *Emotion*, vol. 8(3), pp. 425–9.

9.   Lung Hung Chen and Chia-Huei Wu 2014, 'Gratitude enhances change in athletes' self-esteem', *Journal of Applied Sport Psychology*, vol. 26, issue 3, pp. 349–62.

10. Sheldon, K.M., Todd B. Kashdan, T.B. and Steger, M.F. 2011, *Designing Positive Psychology*, Oxford Press. New York.

11. Kashdan, T.B., Gitendra, U. and Terri, J. 2006, 'Gratitude and hedonic and eudaimonic wellbeing in Vietnam War veterans', *Behaviour Research and Therapy Journal*, vol. 44(2), pp. 177–99.

12. Fredrickson, B. et al., 2003.

13. Emmons, R.A. 2004, *The Psychology of Gratitude*, Oxford University Press, New York.

14. ibid.

15. ibid.

16. Toepfer, S.M. 2012, 'Letters of gratitude: Further evidence for author benefits', *Journal of Happiness Studies*, vol. 13(1), pp. 187–201.

17. ibid.

18. Rickman, C. 2013, *The Flourish Handbook*, Createspace, Scotts Valley, CA.

19. Ling, K. 2013, *Empower Your Day*, accessed at www.kristiling.com

20. Emmons, R.A. 2004.


# 6: Energy and Enjoyment

1. Fredrickson, B. 2009, *Positivity: Ground-breaking research to release your inner optimist and thrive*, Crown, New York.

2. Fry, W. 1971, 'Laughter is the best medicine?' *Stanford MD*, 10.1, pp. 16–20.

3. Buchowski, M.S. 2007, 'Energy expenditure of genuine laughter', *Int J Obes* (Lond), 31(1), pp. 131–7.

4. Provine, R.R. 2000, *Laughter: A scientific research*, Penguin Books. New York.

5. Dunbar, R., Mehu, M. and Little, A. 2007, 'Duchenne smiles and the perception of generosity and sociability in faces', *Journal of Evolutionary Psychology*, 5 (1–4), pp. 133–46.

6. American Physiological Society press release 2009, 'Mirthful laughter, coupled with standard diabetic treatment, raises good cholesterol and may lower heart attack risk'.

7. Lee, B. Tan, D.L., Stanley, A., Bittman, B.B. and Westengard, J. 2001, 'Modulation of neuroimmune parameters during the eustress of humor-associated mirthful laughter', *Alternative Therapies in Health and Medicine*, 7(2), pp. 62–72.

8. American Physiological Society press release 2009.

9. Lee, B. Tan, D.L., Stanley, A., Bittman, B.B. and Westengard, J. 2001.

10. Berk, L. and Tan, S. 1998, 'Humor associated laughter decreases cortisol and increases spontaneous lymphocyte blastogensis', *Clin Res*, 36, p. 435A.

11. Berk, L. and Tan, S. 1995, 'Eustress of mirthful laughter modulates the immune system lymphokine interferon-gama', *Annals of Behavioral Medicine Supplement*, Proceedings of the Society of Behavioral Medicines 16th Annual Scientific Sessions, p. C064.

12. Selye, H. 2012, 'The legacy of Hans Selye and the origins of stress research', *Stress*, 15(5), pp. 472–8.

13. McGhee, P. 2010, *Humor as Survival Training for a Stressed-Out World*, Author House, Bloomington, Indiana.

14. ibid.

15. Fox, K.R. 1999, 'The influence of physical activity on mental wellbeing', *Public Health Nutrition*, 2(3a), pp. 411–18.

16. Smith, T.W. 2006, 'Blood, sweat and tears: Exercise in the management of mental and physical health problems', *Clinical Psychology: Science and Practice, vol.* 13(2), pp. 198–202.

17. Strohle, A. 2009, 'Physical activity, exercise, depression and anxiety disorders', *Journal of Neural Transmission*, pp.116–777.

18. Stubbe, J.H. 2006, 'Regular exercise, anxiety, depression and personality: A population-based study', *Preventive Medicine*, April, vol. 42(4), pp. 273–9.

19. Johnsen, T.J. and Friborg, O. 2015, 'The effects of cognitive behavioral therapy as an anti-depressive treatment is falling: A meta-analysis', *Psychological Bulletin*, accessed at http://dx.doi.org/10.1037/bul0000015

20. O'Conner, P. 2008, 'Low-intensity exercise reduces fatigue symptoms by 65%', *Journal of Psychotherapy and Psychosomatics*, 77(3), pp. 167–74.

## 7: Strengths

1. Linley, P.A., Centre for Confidence and Wellbeing, Positive Psychology Resources, accessed at www.centreforconfidence.co.uk

2. Govindji, R. and Linley, P.A. 2007, 'Strengths use, self-concordance and wellbeing: Implications for strengths coaching and coaching psychologists', *International Coaching Psychology Review*, 2 (2), pp. 143–53.

3. Harter, J.K., Schmidt, F.L. and Hayes, T.L. 2002, 'Business unit level relationship between employee satisfaction, employee engagement, and other business outcomes: A meta-analysis', *Journal of Applied Psychology*, 87, pp. 268–79.

4. Linley, P.A., Centre for Confidence and Wellbeing.

5. Seligman, M. and Peterson, C. 'VIA signature strengths' accessed at www.authentichappiness.sas.upenn.edu

6. Linley, P.A., Centre for Confidence and Wellbeing.

7. www.encylopedia.com Arthur Rubenstein entry

8. Linley, A. 2008, *Average to A+: Realising strengths in yourself and others*, CAPP Press, London.

# Index

## A

ABCDE tool  45–50
acceptance  60–1, 74
action  61
activating events  45–6
activities
    choosing new challenges  109
    everyday mindfulness  114
    to increase happiness  84–5
    listing yours  62–3
    relaxation exercise  103–5
adjustment  61
aggression, reduced  123
altruism  30–1, 112
Alzheimer's disease, pressure of dealing
    with  64–5
anger  143
anxiety  143
appreciation  121–2
attitude
    'completing your circle'  90–1
    defined  75–6
    influence of  91–2
    a positive tool  16
    summing up  95
    task completion  90–1
attitude inventory  92–4
autopilot  98
awareness  60

## B

bed and breakfast business  69–70
behaviours
    iceberg analogy  77–81
    judging others  80
    learned  154
    understanding  76–81
beliefs
    about events  45–6
    disputing  46–7

Berk, Dr Lee  140–2
blood pressure, negativity *vs* positivity
    138

board meetings, initial as CEO  1–3
body surfing experience  105–6
body-based activities  63
brain, parts and function  7–8
brain-based activities  63
breathing exercise  103–4
Broaden and Build theory  13–14
Brown, Dr Brené  59
Buchowski, Professor Maciej  138–9
Buddha, approach to meditation  102

## C

challenges
    creating  107
    setting  109
childhood memories  157
chocolate, focus exercise  112–13
Churchill, Winston  75
circuit breaker, taking a walk  48–9
conclusions, jumping to  66
confidence  69
conflict resolution, between managers
    48–9
conscientiousness  69
cortisol levels, effects of laughter  141
courage  69
creativity, cultivating  30
Csikszentmihalyi, Mihaly  105
curiosity
    health benefits  110
    increasing  118
    nurturing  108–9
    social engagement/happiness  111–12
    supports intelligence  110

meetings
  consequences of disinterest 45
  negative approach to 17
  positive attitude 48
mental health 124
Milne, A.A. 119
mind reading 68
mindfulness
  benefits of 98–100
  curiosity 108–12
  every day activities 114
  intentional attitude 84–5
  large sample group 99
  meditation 101–5
  Now tool 17, 97–8, 112–14
  relaxation exercise 103–5
  savouring the moment 112–14
  summing up 118
  three main qualities 98, 101–2
  walking 128–9
  workplace application 102
Mindfulness Inventory 115–17
mindlessness 98
mindsets
  fixed / growth 85–90
  identifying 88–90
morning cuppa, gratitude routine 129–30
mother's diagnosis, Alzheimer's disease 64
motivation, from curiosity 108–9
movements, automatic 8
multitasking, myth of 100–1
musical instruments, learning 36–7

**N**

negative emotions
  blood pressure 138
  when mind wanders 100
negative energy, sponge effect of 18
negative events, happiness levels 58
negative thoughts, successfully disputed 50
negatives, magnifying 67

neuroplasticity 36–7
non-Duchenne laughter 139–40
Now (mindfulness tool) 17, 97–8, 112–14
Now Inventory 115–17
numbers exercise 89–90

**O**

optimism 35–54
  vs pessimism 36–40
  sign of grit 69
  solution-focused 36
  three dimensions of 37–40
Optimism Inventory 51–3
ORANGES
  explained 23–6
  key differences 25
  name explained 21–2
  research based 26
  seven key principles 25
  toolkit summary 54
  useful tools 26–7
  your approach to 27–8
orders, confirming 42
overgeneralizing 67–8

**P**

pain tolerance, increased 30
past, thinking about 101
permanence
  challenging 42
  explained 37
  understanding 38–9
personal strengths
  categories 154–5
  defined 151
  playing to our 19–20
  practise to improve 156–7
  Strengths Inventory 159–62
  summing up 163
  tips for spotting 157–8
  understanding 153–5

## U

## V

## W